What others are saying about this book:

"A beneficial, compact, and informative source book.....Well organized and full of hard facts, helpful hints, and pertinent resources....Recommended for all who wish to save time and money when placing a personal ad."

"One of the most comprehensive, readable, and definitive manuals on the market today on how to find a date/mate."

"An indispensable manual for those who want to broaden their lives."

WARNING - DISCLAIMER

This book is designed to provide information in regard to the subject matter covered. It is sold with the understanding that the publisher and author are not engaged in rendering legal or other professional services. If legal or other expert assistance is required, the services of a competent professional should be sought.

The purpose of this manual is to educate and entertain. The author and Baron Publications shall have neither liability nor responsibility to any person or entity with respect to any loss or damage caused, or alleged to be caused, directly or indirectly by the information contained in this book.

If you do not desire to be bound by the above, you may return this book to the publisher for a full refund.

PERSONAL ADS --

NEVER BE LONELY AGAIN

Author
Marlene Halbig

Editor
Barbara Vaine

Baron Publications, Laguna Beach, California

PERSONAL ADS - NEVER BE LONELY AGAIN

I lovingly dedicate this book to my husband Fred and our children: Bruce, Carole, Janet, John, Julie, Ted, and their families.

ACKNOWLEDGEMENTS

Without the faith and support of my family and friends who believed in me, this book may never have been written. Many people were helpful, but especially:

Charles T. Miles for allowing me to use his splendid Grin Graphics.

Dr. James H. Johnson for his permission to use his fascinating software program, What-If Compatibility Prober.

Frederick J. Halbig who has trust in me.

Barbara and Paul Vaine who accept me, and encouraged me to share my story, and who spent a great deal of time reviewing and editing the manuscript.

Rosalie Winston who helped me laugh my way to getting this book going, and then shared in the editing process.

Charles McCoy for his coaching and Raymond Hernandez for his recommendations and superlative forms.

Michael Callahan for his excellent art work on the cover and last page of Chapter Four.

Jarrod L. Reed for his patience and understanding when we asked for "one more" edit and for his wizardry in computer typesetting the book.

TABLE OF CONTENTS

A WORD FROM THE AUTHOR

As a single person you may have experienced the loneliness of spending an evening by yourself when the company of a friend, especially a date, becomes an aching desire. Most humans need companionship, love, tenderness and the attention of a special person, whether a lover, friend or companion.

This book originated with my own need for someone to help me over the "rough spots" and to keep me from being lonely. As my children grew to maturity and left home for their own lives, I realized that someone was needed to replace them. They couldn't actually be replaced, but I definitely needed someone with whom I could talk, laugh, plan, love, romance, and who would take loneliness from my life.

Since I had been away from the singles scene for so long I was leery of doing the usual bar scenes, singles clubs, "meat markets", etc. Also, I was very security conscious and the lack of control over the meeting process was very scary. I needed a method to screen the men who might become an important part of my life so that only those who had the attributes I wanted would be accepted. And the "personals" worked!

My wish is that you enjoy reading this book and, more importantly, enjoy using the "personals" to enrich your life and to "never be lonely again". Write me about your experiences and questions - - I would love to hear from you.

INTRODUCTION

WHAT THIS BOOK WILL DO FOR YOU

You will learn:

Today's Lesson

PERSONAL ADS

How To

How to *produce* a captivating personal ad to attract your ideal date/mate by using my easy step-by-step system.

The secrets of how to *cull* your responses in order to filter out the undesirable in minutes.

How to *manage* letters, phone calls, and dates - removing the apprehensions of dating.

How to easily *select* the right publications and how to *respond* to personal ads.

THE NUMBERS GAME

Imagine dating 75 men all within one year - just to find NUMBER ONE! But if you think that's mind boggling, I was willing to screen as many as it took to find Mr. Right - even if the screening ran into the hundreds or thousands! But I didn't have to do that because I learned the secret of the "Key Word" technique. And I'm going to share the secret with you!

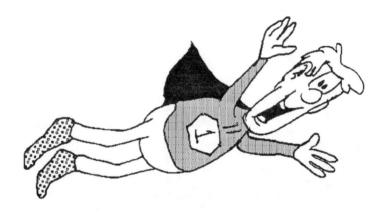

Use the "Key Word" system, and your dream person will come to you - with all the specified traits.

By narrowing down your search, you can be successful within a very short time. I know! It happened to me! After being contacted by 75 potential dates (20 of whom I actually met), one man turned out to be a very special person in my life.

Personal ads for meeting people is not a new concept. Advertising for a date/mate on a large scale has been around since before the 60's. The 80's saw date/mate personal ads take off. Now into the 90's, the ads have arrived!

WORD CHOICE CAN HAVE UNEXPECTED RESULTS

Most people have the ability to write ads to sell an automobile, a refrigerator, or even a house. But when you write a personal ad, you're selling yourself and describing the parameters of what you expect in return - all in 50 words or less. Although each word in your ad is important, some words are *crucial*.

For example, in one of my ads, I described myself as "into fitness." What I meant to convey was that I was in good physical shape and into health. I didn't mention marathon running, weight lifting, triathalons (all of which I'm not into) and in truth my only exercises are my weekly aerobics class and walking.

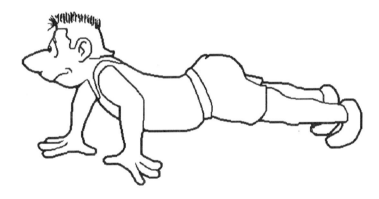

Well, was I surprised to receive responses from body builders, runners, etc., who couldn't wait to get with me to train together for their particular sporting event.

The lesson I learned was to choose my words very carefully, so as not to waste the time of others - not to mention my own. Therefore, in my next ad I wrote "healthy, trim, and fit" and was able to convey just what I wanted: Namely, "I am slim, into health (no junk food), do moderate exercise, and expect that those who answer my ad to have the same mindset."

EVERYONE IS DOING IT!!

You may be wondering - "If it's so wonderful, why isn't everyone doing it?" Well, they are - NEARLY EVERYBODY! Millions of personal ads are published everyday in just about every conceivable publication across the country! Finally, for the first time in history people are getting together and not feeling they are taking pot-luck. They are getting to know each other because they want to! With the personal ads you specify whom you want to meet - No others!

Well, then, if so many are doing it, does this include your family and friends? They may not have told you they were meeting all new and interesting people through the personal ads. But I'm sure some of them have and oftentimes feel a little uncomfortable telling people about advertising for a date/mate.

Why not lead the way? Just mention you are considering placing a personal ad; then, sit back and listen. In most cases, your family and friends will share their experiences of reading, responding, or writing ads for a date/mate.

THEY ARE DOING IT ON THE TELEPHONE!

Many publications are accepting ads that are responded to by voice mail rather than through the post office. One such publication, *The Orange County Preview*, has a section titled, "Affection Connection." Along with a free Affection Connection ad, you receive a free "Voice Mailbox" - a phone service allowing you to record and receive messages from any touch-tone phone.

THIS IS HOW YOU DO IT:

1.   PLACE YOUR AD

Complete the ad form they supply and mail or FAX to the Affection Connection. The first 25 words are free; additional words cost 50 cents each. Ads run for a maximum of 4 weeks. The Affection Connection assigns you a 4-digit private security code for exclusive access to your responses.

2.   USE YOUR VOICE MAILBOX

After you receive your mailbox number and private security code, you can record your personal introduction in order to tell the listener more about yourself.

3.   LISTEN TO YOUR RESPONSES

You are given a 1-800 number, which is available 24 hours a day, to listen to your responses.

The Affection Connection is available to any person seeking a sincere relationship. They will not accept ads containing explicit or implicit sexual-anatomical language, or offering anything of monetary value - living accommodations, gifts, or trips in exchange for companionship. You must be 18 years of age or older, and no ads will be accepted from advertisers seeking relationships with persons under the age of 18.

4.   RESPONSE

Although responding to the Voice Mailbox is great because you don't have to wait for the mail to be delivered, it costs the respondent 98 cents a minute. All you do is dial a 1-900 number and recorded messages instruct you on your choices. If you don't want to respond to a specific ad, there are recordings by men or women whom you may listen to.

THE RICH AND FAMOUS ARE DOING IT!

Recently, at a very chic cocktail party, I met Karen, a gorgeous, wealthy, Newport Beach socialite. The conversation evolved to the point of my writing this book, and she confided in me that she had become very bored with the local dating scene - "Handsome, glib, wealthy, young men in expensive, fast automobiles who were going nowhere."

It seems even though she was born into money, sent to the best schools, had the most beautiful trendy clothes, and made the social scenes of Southern California, she still hadn't met the right man. Karen belonged to many philanthropic organizations and was gifted with a doting family and many wonderful friends who introduced her to numerous eligible bachelors. She knew Mr. Right was out there and if she met enough men, she would find him. Karen is a business woman, and she decided to put her business skills to work.

When you fish for love, bait with your heart, not your brain.

Mark Twain

KEY WORD SYSTEM PUT TO WORK

First, she made a list of the qualifications she would like to have in a mate. From her list (she was surprised to find 50 items), she created a "must" list - things she must have in her mate - which included 5 items: S/W/M, tall, successful, N/S, and monogamous.

Second, she answered a couple of personal ads that fit her "must" list. She found that even though the men had met the qualifications, it wasn't enough - the men weren't fitting in with "who she was." Therefore, she decided in the future to take a proactive role (in other words, take charge of her life).

Third, she made a list of words that described who she is and placed a personal ad with a local, upscale, business publication using Voice Mail for its personal ads. Her ad:

> "Attractive European blonde, S/W/F, 35, tall, slim. Incurable romantic, playful, intelligent, sophisticated, and happy. Seeks tall, successful, N/S, S/W/M for exciting relationship and lifelong, happiness."

Fourth, she left a message on her Voice Mail that further instructed the respondents to write her a letter describing themselves and to send a photo.

SUCCESS

Karen received 35 responses. She was overwhelmed, but more than overwhelmed, she was thrilled with the quality of men who had replied. She carefully screened her responses and discovered Kevin, the man of her dreams. (Kevin's story is in Chapter Three, "Responding to the Personals.")

SPREADING THE WORD

Now Karen is sharing her "secret" with her friends and family - giving advice on how to get more out of life by not being alone.

BEAUTY SALON MATCH-UP

A California beauty salon is offering its customers more than just a new look - it also wants to provide someone to admire it. After years of informal matching, the owner has added a dating service to the long list of services available at her shop. In keeping with Los Angeles tradition, the matchmaking is a little offbeat. To give patrons a more personal and spiritual approach to dating, the owner has the patrons spend 10 minutes with the salon's psychic advisor and complete a 10-page questionnaire. The counseling "gives people a deeper look at themselves and what they're looking for," according to the salon's promotional literature. As with conventional dating services, each potential lovebird is invited in to look at photographs and relevant information about potential partners. Enrollees are charged $35 per introductory meeting.

SOME ARE DOING IT WITH PICTURES AND VOICE MAIL

For $129. a small local publication publishes ads with your picture ($99. without the picture), for a three-month listing. This allows the caller to see what you look like, read your message, and call a private 24-hour-message center. The caller will hear your private greeting and leave a private message for you. There are no fees to the calling party, and no additional fees to you - no matter how often you use the system to access your messages. The concept is good, and the price is not out of line. However, be very selective when you put your picture in for publication - some of the pictures look like police line-up mug shots.

COMMUTERS ARE DOING IT!

Another way to advertise for a mate or date in Southern California is the brain child of a Huntington Beach entrepreneur. He developed the concept of

"Commuter Dating Connections," while commuting to work. It came to him that since motorists spend a lot of time in traffic, why not use the time well. He printed decals and brochures and secured a 900 number.

Membership in the program is $19.95 for three months for which members receive a red - trimmed decal for their car window. It gets right to the point: "Commuter Dating Connections, 900-505-CALL!" and an extension number. Members also have use of a Voice Mail message system and can receive a newsletter.

THEY ARE DOING IT ON CABLE TV

Television personals are other options for meeting friends, companions and, just possibly, finding romance. Your ad is read aloud as the words are shown on the

screen to the musical strains of love-themes or light jazz. Serving as backgrounds, are pictures of romantic settings such as fields of flowers, woodsy roads, misty mountains, quaint bridges, sailboats, and lots of waterfalls. The more self-assured may substitute photographs of themselves.

EXPENDITURES FOR THE AD PLACER

The cost for the TV ad placer is not expensive: $50 per ad of 50 words or less for a one-week run. And according to the article I read, the response is great.

EXPENDITURES FOR RESPONDENTS

But it can get expensive for interested respondents. A telephone number is shown on the screen and for $2.70 a minute, callers hear the recorded voice of the object of their interest and have an opportunity to leave their own phone numbers.

As you can see there are many ways to help you get together with interesting people - and that is what this book is all about!

NOW IT'S TIME FOR YOU TO DO IT!

CHAPTER ONE

THE AD

THE BOTTOM LINE

Love, happiness, relationship, companionship, marriage, dating, dancing...they can all be yours through the personal ads!

The techniques of getting started, writing the ad, knowing where to send it, and weeding out responses will unfold as you read this chapter.

Through personal experience, interviews, and research, the material was organized to create a simplified working model of the Ad Questionnaire which you can use time and time again with slight modifications to get the results you want - fast!

I have included five Ad Questionnaires for your use. (See Appendix, Form section.) After you have read this chapter, which contains the Ad Questionnaire example, go to the form section and tear out one of the forms and follow along with the instructions.

MOBILIZE

Before we get into the ad, there are several items that you will need when the responses come in.

1.   A post office (P.O.) box is a must! Because of paperwork, most post offices have a waiting period of several weeks before they are able to issue a P.O. box. Meanwhile, if you have placed your ad before you apply for a P.O. box, and you want to correspond with your respondents, there won't be an address that they can write to. You don't give your home address to strangers, do you? And at this point the respondents are strangers, aren't they? Always exercise <u>caution</u> in giving out your address until you are confident of your respondents' intentions. (See Chapter Two for more on safety precautions.)

2.   Thank-you notes or any type of note paper and envelopes. When those responses come in, you don't want to have to scramble around for something to write on.   (See Chapter Two for corresponding with the respondents.)

3.   Postage stamps. Postage stamp needs go without saying.

WHERE SHOULD YOU PLACE YOUR AD?

READ! REVIEW! READ!

You can save yourself money if, before you place your ad, you read and review other ads. (See Appendix for "Imaginative Ads For Reviewing.")

GENERIC READING

What type of publication do you generally read? A relaxing pastime for me is reading the local entertainment guides. A major portion of these guides is devoted to common interest advertisements (personal ads). Do review the entire publication, not just the ads. Your review should give you some insight into what type of readership it attracts. Would the type of readership be people you'd want to spend time with? Then, become familiar with these ads and the publication charges.

SPECIALIZED READING

Instead of reading generic-type publications, you may prefer more specialized reading; such as magazines on art, music, food, wine, business, or health.

Or specialized newspapers - e.g., for senior citizens, or pilots. Newsletters are available on every conceivable subject including: fishing, hunting, baseball, RV camping. Almost all run personal ads (even if they don't now, they probably will in the near future). Look for ads that give enough information for you to decide if you're interested in meeting the authors. These publications charge the least for common interest ads. The circulation may not be as wide, but if you are focusing on a certain group - for example, The Square Dancers of San Francisco - this would be a good way for you to go.

Take love away from life and you take away its pleasure.
                                                    Jean Baptiste Moliere

CITIZEN OF THE WORLD

Then again, if you are the cosmopolitan type, you may choose to run your ad in a metropolitan newspaper. The per word costs will be high, but the readership could run into the hundreds of thousands. I don't consider myself much of a cosmopolitan. Nevertheless, I ran an ad in one such publication for three days and it was very expensive. Although I did receive a good response, 35 replies, all were very diverse and contradictory to what I was looking for. Many of those who responded were far more sophisticated in the affairs of the heart than I, and it made me feel uncomfortable just reading their responses.

It is better to have loved and lost than never to have loved at all.

Alfred, Lord Tennyson

ROMANCE AND CYRANO DE BERGERAC

However, being the romantic that I am, I overcame being uncomfortable, and read every word. For instance, one letter writer opened his letter with a short introduction describing several interests he felt we had in common (taken from my ad). Then he went on to describe himself as "very sincere, loving, romantic, caring, understanding and highly sensitive to music and romance. A man who is anxious to share the goodness of life, the ideals, the plans for a better future with that special woman close to me." He went on to further describe himself, and then he closed his letter with: "This is a small view of an inner part of my soul and feelings. Still, there is more, much more that I would like to share with you."

I did correspond via the telephone with my romantic letter writer, but as it turned out - after several telephone conversations - the man with all the soul who wrote the letter and the man with whom I spoke were not one and the same.

DOCTOR, LAWYER, INDIAN CHIEF

The metropolitan newspaper in which I placed one of my ads isn't considered sophisticated, but the readership is diverse and therefore, so may be the ad authors and ad respondents. Out of the 35 persons who answered my ad, there were accountants, a movie director (possibly retired), real estate salesmen, consultants, actors, defense workers, probation officers, retirees, a lawyer, a doctor, and at least two blatant gigolos.

What is love? I have met in the streets a very poor young man who was in love. His hat was old, his coat worn, the water passed through his shoes and the stars through his soul.

Victor Hugo

FREE! FREE! FREE!

If you don't subscribe to many publications and if you are interested in placing an ad in a publication that would bring in diverse types of respondents, use your local public library. Review the magazines and newspapers and browse through the personal ads to determine if you feel comfortable with the ad authors.

The ad costs are generally listed and may sway your decision as to whether you want to place your ad in that type of publication. For example, the last time I checked the *New York* magazine, which runs ads nationwide, charged around $29 per line (36 characters in a line.)

The longest ad I read (written by a woman) contained 30 lines! By the time I finished reading her ad I knew exactly what she was looking for, and none others need apply. I doubt that she received many replies because there wasn't room for flexibility in her ad. It's too bad because had she been more flexible and received a larger response, she could have done her screening later. In that same issue the average ad was eight lines and got the message across without eliminating the entire universe. It's okay to focus on what you want, but be realistic!

OVERWHELMED

My ad in the metropolitan newspaper was my first attempt to find someone with common interests, so I wasn't prepared for 35 responses. They arrived over a period of two weeks and I kept busy trying to contact respondents and then keeping them straight. Once I realized the trouble I was in, trying to keep the respondents names and personal information matched, I devised a crude check and balance system.

THE SYSTEM: keeping all the personal information I had gleaned from our conversations on the envelope in which they had sent their original letter, and keeping all the envelopes near the telephone.

SEEING TRIPLE

Things were going fairly well with my system until three Kens answered my ad. During the course of correspondence and telephone calls, one of the them would call and say, "Hi, this is Ken." At first I would panic and try to get Ken to talk so I could figure out which Ken was on the other end. My obvious dilemma was that if Ken knew I had more than one Ken to choose from, it might be a turn off in our getting to know each other. But the panic didn't last long because I simply began the conversation by asking for his last name or some significant information so that I could remember which one he was.

By the way, none of the Kens and I ever got together. Two of the Kens loved to talk on the phone; in fact, one Ken called me two or three times a week for a month or so. However, each time I tried to arrange a meeting, he would have to cancel. I don't know how long this would have gone on if I hadn't finally told him I had met someone special and therefore didn't feel we should continue to correspond. Even though it wasn't quite the truth, it is a kind way to let others down who have proven they really don't want to meet you in person. They are lonely and only want someone to talk with.

I ran the same ad (with slight variations) in a publication with specialized interests, which I found appealing. I received 40 responses, and almost half were those with whom I could relate.

RV CAMPERS WANTED

When I ran one of my ads, I didn't mention RV camping. Instead, I wrote "weekend trips" and received a number of responses from men who had RVs - all set up and ready to roll. Although I haven't had the opportunity to do much RV traveling, I can attest to the fact, ladies, that if you are in to it, there are a lot of men out there waiting to hear from you!

BE SPECIFIC

In my ad I was too general when I listed "weekend trips" as one of my interests. What I meant was I liked to travel, but had little time. My intended trips were for destinations within a one to two hour airplane trip away from home. And because those excursions were important to me, I should have been more specific. Perhaps, "air travel to weekend get-a-ways?"

COME OUT AND PLAY

One of my respondents interpreted my "weekend trips" to mean something completely off base from what I was trying to get across. When he responded to my ad, he offered trips that would include Mexico and Hawaii - all to be paid by him. He missed the point entirely because further into my ad I said I was looking for a long-term relationship. He may not have interpreted my ad correctly - but I fully understood his intent.

BONUS

One of the shopper-type publications in my area offers a bonus if you will read their common interest ads each week looking for the most clever ad. When you feel you have found the ad, you mail it to their paper and you may win dinner for two. Another publication states that if you find your mate through a personal ad in their paper, you will receive a night-on-the-town including dinner for two at an elegant restaurant.

Since you will be studying ads anyway, you may want to look for those publications which offer rewards for reading their ads.

THAT PERSON COULD BE YOU

 Ad reading is much like ad writing. You'll find yourself matching up personality traits with what the authors describe about themselves or for the requirements they ask for. Soon you'll be saying to yourself, "I could be that person, or I'm the person they are looking for." (If the latter is the case, read Chapter Three, "Responding to the Personals," to determine if you are ready to respond to an ad.)

From your research you can determine the commonality between you and the authors. Therefore, you need not look any further. If the ad authors closely reflect your own tastes and social preferences, that is the publication for you!

ACKNOWLEDGEMENT

When someone takes the time to respond to your ad, use common courtesy! Acknowledge him/her as soon as possible. So, if you receive many responses and are unable to call, then send them a short thank you note, giving them some idea when you will call. (*Always keep your word!*)

REJECTION

Those respondents whom you never expect to call should get the same courtesy. Except when writing a thank you note, let them know that you won't be getting in touch. Statements such as: "Thank you for writing, you seem very likeable, but I have recently met someone I'm interested in."

BE TACTFUL

Remember you are dealing with a person's psyche. Despite the use of tact, you're still rejecting them. Therefore, tell them something they can live with: for example, "I liked your letter, but I've already made a commitment." Or "I was fascinated with your lifestyle; unfortunately, mine is quite different."

CONSIDERATE

But even beyond the courtesy acknowledgement, is the awareness that someone read your ad and thinks that you are special enough to write to. That same person must have thought he or she was somewhat special too, and therefore took the initiative in writing. If you don't acknowledge the response, there is almost a certainty that this individual will suffer some feeling of rejection.

WORKING MODEL

The following Ad Questionnaire is in three steps.

1. Just who are you?
2. What are you looking for?
3. The sum of the whole equals one clear, concise, great ad.

Notice that I have filled in the blanks for you (I did say it was a working model). After you have read over the questions and answers, grab a pen, pull out an Ad Questionnaire from the Appendix, Form section, and fill in the blanks.

THE AD QUESTIONNAIRE - STEP ONE
JUST WHO ARE YOU?

1.   Marital Status: a) Single _✓_ b) Divorced _____
c) Widow/Widower _____ d) Never Married_____
There isn't a whole lot of difference between a) and b) above, but the
trend appears to be to use a); it has a more positive ring to it.

2.   Ethnic Group _W_____

3.   Sex _F_ This is not a yes/no question, so enter the first initial M or F.

4.   Vital statistics: a) Age _30½_ b) Height _5'3"_ c) Weight _110_

5.   Describe your physical and mental attributes in five positive words or less.
a) _bright_   b) _caring_
c) _energetic_   d) _fun-loving_
e) _romantic_

Remember! Honesty is very important when describing yourself. However, you
can be easy on yourself. If for example, you are uncomfortable stating in your ad
(for all the world to read) that you are 47 years of age, then say 40ish. If you are
male, 5'5" and weigh 160 pounds, state your height and describe yourself as stocky,
or teddybearish - not stating your actual weight. Or if you are a woman with those
same dimensions, state your height, but describe yourself as an armful, or
huggable, or rounded.

TO TELL THE TRUTH

Always be **positive**, but don't stretch the truth too far when describing yourself. You may get hundreds of responses to your ad if you portray yourself as a Tom Selleck or a Marilyn Monroe look-a-like, but what will happen when you meet the respondents face-to-face? Surprise!

A case in point could be that you are uncomfortably overweight. You know that you are a desirable, warm, and wonderful person, and many men and women prefer the overweight. But think carefully about the way you want to be represented. Words such as "a loving, huggable, armful", "great things do come in large packages", or "something to hold on to" are positive ways to describe your situation. Or list your actual height/weight. But be honest! If you aren't you may be setting yourself up for rejection. Another choice is placing your ad in a special publication designed for the overweight.

THE REAL YOU...OR A CLOSE PROXIMITY THEREOF

The same goes for any information on your vital statistics. Be kind to yourself but be **honest!!** This cannot be stressed enough. When I met with the respondents to my ad, most told me they had experienced more than one difficult encounter. Some said, "I'm pleasantly surprised your self-description so closely matches up with the real you." Others went on to relate how quickly they made their exit after meeting ad-placers who weren't so honest.

6.   List, in their order of importance, hobbies and sports in which you participate on a regular basis:

   a) Hobbies ___*rock music*___

   b) Sports ___*tennis*___

The importance of listing the above is that those who respond to your ad will share the common interest. For example, if your hobbies and sports all center around the water - such as scuba diving, surfing, and water polo - this will eliminate those potential respondents who prefer horseback riding, bungie cord jumping, and hang gliding. Of course, if respondents are flexible and adventurous, investigating new hobbies and pastimes may be just what they are looking for, and you both may benefit from getting together.

Love sought is good, but given unsought is better.

                                    William Shakespeare

NO COMPROMISE

7.   List those things that are a must in your life.

"Musts" may include children, pets, or being a regular churchgoer. Some essentials can be worked out in a compromise, such as morning person vs. night person. It is important, however, to list whatever is significant to you and if those who respond feel they can negotiate any differences, then you both will benefit. But if you don't state what is of uppermost importance to you in your ad, when it comes out in your new relationship (and it will), problems may develop.

"MUSTS": *must like children*

THE AD QUESTIONNAIRE - STEP TWO
WHAT ARE YOU LOOKING FOR?

8.   Put a check mark in the box that best describes what you're looking for in a relationship:

a) Marriage ✔   b) Romance ____   c) Friendship ____

d) Companionship ____   e) Come-Out-and-Play ____

f) Something else ____

If your choice is "something else" (for example, you may be looking for a second for bridge or a square dance partner), this book can still help you because all the information is not just for romance; it is also a means of helping you find out who you really are.

Also, if you are unsure of what type of relationship you want, then Item f) is a good choice. It may limit your responses, but it will focus on at least one characteristic or talent that you would like to share with someone. And if you are hesitant in getting into a relationship, this will be an ideal approach to find out if you want to go further.

For Item f) a good example of an ad for a dance partner is:

"2 left feet S/W/M 35, looking for dance partner with similar foot problems and/or patience to take private dance lessons and occasional night of dancing. Partner social country western lessons on flexible schedule. All lessons paid. Not seeking relationship."

FOUR QUALITIES

9.   What are the four most important
         qualities you're looking for in the person
         you want the relationship with? Use one
         to four words (if possible) to describe
         those attributes.   If you are male, the
         qualities most important to you in a
         woman could be: "attractive, caring, warm
         and romantic." If you are a woman, they
         might be: "honest, sincere, financially
         secure, and witty."

a) *non-smoker*

b) *honest*

c) *warm*

d) *humorous*

ROUNDING IT OUT

There may be types of people whom you would prefer to date. Make a check mark or fill in the blank, as applicable.

10. Ethnic group: a) Caucasian ✓ b) Black ____

c) Hispanic ____ d) Oriental ____

e) Does not matter_____

f) Other, specify _____

11. Age range ___*30 - 50*_____

12. Height range ___*5'5" to 6'*_____

13. Dating a smoker is: a) Okay ____ b) Not okay ✓

c) Does not matter ____

14. Dating a social drinker is: a) Okay ✓

b) Not okay____ c) Does not matter ____

> In dreams and love, there are no impossibilities.
> Janos Arany

JUST THE FACTS MA'AM

Now that you have completed the Ad Questionnaire (Steps One and Two), you know who you are and what you want, and now it's time to organize/market the material. I prefer the informational style of marketing.

If you are witty and clever you may prefer the creative ad, and you will probably attract people who think as you do. To simplify the process for now, however, use the informational style below as your model.

THE AD QUESTIONNAIRE - STEP THREE
YOUR AD

15. Me: SWF 30's, 5'3" 110 Lbs. Bright, caring, energetic, fun loving, romantic. Collects rock music. Love tennis. You: SWM, likes children/LTR, honest, humorous, warm, 30-50, 5'5"- 6', N/S, social drinker ok.

You have selected your publication and you have your ad, now go for it!

CHAPTER TWO

FILTERING YOUR RESPONSES

THE FUN BEGINS

When you go to your mail box and see it is stuffed with mail forwarded to you from the newspaper where you placed your ad - the excitement begins!

But don't lose your cool! Before you start ripping open those envelopes, grab this manual, a pen, and tear out one of the checklists provided for you in the back of this book (see Appendix, Form section).

Follow along with the instructions below. The instructions walk you through your responses, and I have provided you with enough checklists for 18 responses.

By the time you have answered 18 letters, you will probably have some ideas of your own on what to add to the checklist to personalize it.

> We are all born for love: it is the principle of existence and its only end.
>
> Benjamin Disraeli

INSTRUCTIONS FOR COMPLETING RESPONSE FORM

Note: The instructions below take you through the full form completion cycle for the first letter that you receive.   Repeat the instructions for each succeeding letter.

BEGIN NOW

Line 1.   Identify each envelope with a big number 1, 2, and so forth; enter the same number on Line 1. Enter the date you received the response - now you can rip open the envelope.

Line 2.   Note anything unusual. For example, if the person is totally off base as to what you stated in the ad (you may have said you wanted to meet someone who was willing to travel year round and a non-smoker, and they replied they were home-bodies who chain smoked), then note it.

Line 3.   Enter the person's name, address, and phone number.

Line 4.   Enter the person's age, height, and weight.

Line 5.   On the average, that is the most information you'll receive with this first letter. However, if there is other pertinent information, this is where it goes. For example, the respondent may state he/she is a Christian or regular churchgoer (you may be an agnostic).

Complete Lines 6 through 11 while you are making the call to your respondent.

BEFORE YOU CALL

Some things you don't tell people on
your first call:

YOUR LAST NAME,
YOUR HOME ADDRESS,
AND YOUR WORK
PHONE NUMBER.
Remember, you are still in
the response screening
process, and you don't know
if the person on the other end of the line is as warm and wonderful as
you.

FOREWARD PLANNING - THE MEETING PLACE

For security and convenience, now is the time to decide where you will meet your
favored respondents. Geographically speaking, you will have to know something
about their location in relation to where you live. Some personal ads state
specifically that readers need not apply if they don't live within a certain city,
county, or square mile radius from a certain point. I didn't place location
restrictions in my ads, but I did get replies from 100 miles away and more. (I
never got together with anyone who was more than 50 miles from my home base.)
So if you don't want to go out of your area to meet people, then state it in your ad.

> To live without love is not really to live.
>
> Jean Baptiste Moliere

PLACES TO MEET - USE CAUTION

Before I met with my potential date/mates I researched well-lit coffee shops or restaurants. Although not very imaginative, I felt safe in meeting my respondents in those type of places and also I wasn't distracted by outside influences - such as if we had met in a zoo or art gallery. The point is the meeting place is your call. If you allow the other person to set the rendezvous, you pass some of the control to the other person. Regardless of who makes the arrangements, visit the place beforehand to be sure you will be comfortable. If you aren't, change locations!

BE PREPARED WITH THE BOX NUMBER

Many times the respondents have answered more than one ad, so they may ask you for the box number or identification number under which the newspaper placed your ad. Keep the number by the phone!

> All's fair in love and war.
>
> Francis Smedley

RELAX

If you are like me, making the first call will really be a big event. Just thinking of doing it would make my palms break out in perspiration and - to make matters worse - my voice would crack and my mind go blank. So before I dialed the number, I held a rehearsal.

REHEARSAL TIME

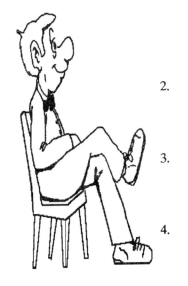

1. Select a quiet and relaxing time. Refrain from making calls when others are in the house or when other interruptions are possible.

2. Seat yourself in a comfortable chair near the telephone. (Sit up straight.)

3. Put a smile on your face (the smile will come through in your voice).

4. Take a couple of deep breaths to steady yourself, pick-up the telephone, and imagine you are making the call. Yes, I said imagine.

PRACTICE

With telephone in hand, rehearse speaking slowly. If you have a speaking problem (anxious hemming and hawing, or other verbal stumbling) pull out a tape-recorder and tape yourself in ordinary conversation. Speak as if following a script until you are comfortable with the opening line: "Hello, I'd like to speak with Beverly." When your party gets on the line, open your conversation by referring to something in your ad your respondent mentioned in his or her letter as shown in th following example:

> Your ad may have opened with, "Tennis bum looking for a partner," and the respondent may have referred to tennis in the letter.

> You say, "Hi Beverly, I'm the tennis bum you wrote to."

Now you are ready for the first call, and completing Lines 6 through 11.

MAKING THE CALL.

Dial the number and if you are lucky, a human being will answer. However, if a machine answers, use your most congenial voice and greet your respondent by name, state who you are, your number, and time that is best to return your call. The last two items are optional because you pass some of the control over to him/her when you leave your number. Also, you may feel obligated to stay near the phone if you leave the hours when to call. I always liked to be the initiator of the calls; that way I could select a time when I was available. It is not necessary to mention the purpose.

GETTING THROUGH THE INTRODUCTION

Providing you get your party on the line, introduce yourself and state you are responding to their letter. Always ask if the person has a few minutes to talk. If the answer is "Yes," start the conversation with the items from lines 6 through 10. You can start at any point using the form as a prompt. Most of the information will come out in normal give-and-take dialogue.

Complete Lines 6 through 10 in a natural conversational manner - not as if you were conducting a job interview. You are developing a preliminary profile of someone who would like to get together with you in the near future; so these little bits of information woven together will give you a good idea if this individual is someone with whom you will want to spend some of your valuable time.

LINES 6 THROUGH 10

Line 6. Cultural Interests: Theater ____ Dance ____ Music ____
Visual Arts____Film ____

Line 7. Marital Status: Never married ____ Divorced ____
Widow ____Widower ____

Line 8. Children: Has ____ Hasn't ____ Desires ____ No opinion ____

Line 9. Religious or non-religious preference: Protestant ____ Catholic ____
Jewish____Agnostic ____ Atheist ____ Other _____

Line 10. Education: 4-year College _____ Advanced Degree _____

Other _____

When you have completed Lines 1 through 10, you will have a profile of your respondent. Now it is RATING TIME.

Line 11. Rating: Excellent _____ Good _____ Forget It _____

Add any personal notes: _____

_____

TO MEET OR NOT TO MEET

Once you have rated the respondent (Line 11) you should have a good idea whether you want to set up a meeting. Now you have choices to make:

1. Do you want to meet right away? Then, set up the meeting.

2. Do you want to screen your respondent further? Tell him/her you would like to call back and talk some more at a later date.

3. Do you want to end it here? Well then.....

DON'T MINCE WORDS! SAY WHAT YOU MEAN!

This is the uncomfortable part of filtering responses. You probably won't want to meet every respondent you talk to. Out of the 75 responses I received, I only met 20. If you feel for any reason that you aren't interested in meeting, tell him/her so. But be kind (remember the psyche). Just say you don't feel you share enough common interests. Wish him/her luck...and that's all you need to say!

THE FIRST MEETING

1. You have selected a public, well-lit place with which you are familiar. Remember to use CAUTION - the person you are about to meet is a stranger. Do NOT meet in a private home. Do NOT go to a private residence with the respondent on the first meeting - or ever - if you haven't checked him/her out.

    One of the ways I investigated my respondents was to exchange work phone numbers. I would call at work to say thanks for a pleasant evening, or they would call me.

2. Tell a friend where you will be and when you expect to be back.

    If you are going to be late, give your friend a phone call. If you have no one to tell, then jot down the pertinent information (the name and phone number of the person whom you are meeting and where you will be meeting) and leave it in an easy-to-locate area in your home (kitchen table, refrigerator door, or dresser mirror).

3.   Exercise CAUTION. Drive in separate cars both before and after you meet. If you have any doubts about someone, walk away from the encounter.

Of the 20 men I met from using the personals, one was a little strange, but all were more than polite and treated me as if I were very special. I value intuition (inner voice) and I listened to mine. I found it easier to get a picture of someone while we were still in the telephone calling stage. The voice is much like looking into the soul because you don't have all the distractions associated with in-person meetings.   If your intuition is a little rusty, brush up on it. Your local library is a good source for books on intuition.

THE LADY IN THE RED DRESS

When the meeting place is agreed upon, establish some way your respondents will identify you and you them. A red rose behind your ear? Well, you get the idea.

> It is a beatiful necessity of our nature to love something.
>
> Douglas Jerrold

SCREEN! SCREEN! SCREEN!

The first meeting may be the turning point of your life. It was for me. But no matter how great your first impression is, continue to screen. Be alert to body language, dress style, conversation and sense of humor. Even with all these clues, the most important factors for me are: "Do I feel comfortable with him, and do we have some chemistry going?" Those are observations only you will feel and know. So let's move on.

THE INITIAL DATE DRAWS TO A CLOSE

Who pays? Go dutch! Unless, of course, you are so smitten with your date and loaded with dough; then offer to pay.

PICK ME!

Millions of words have been written about "rejection" and all the unhappiness that goes with it; therefore, for this book, I won't elaborate on this subject. However, I will say since you are in control, your responsibility is to reject someone with as much kindness as possible - it will make a difference!

LEAVE 'EM LAUGHING

Always leave your dates with a positive feeling about the meeting and about themselves. Whether you screen them in or screen them out, concentrate on some positive aspect of their personality, their looks, their clothes, and tell them about it.

SCREENED OUT

"I've really enjoyed our getting together. You're an interesting person, but I don't think we share enough common interests to meet again." Then make a quick exit. Or if you really can't stand hurting someone and there may be a glimmer of interest, say something like, "I've really enjoyed meeting with you and would like to take a week or so to think things over." Then do think things over and if you know you won't be seeing that person again, send a thank-you note.

SCREENED IN

"I've had a great time tonight. You have an outstanding sense of humor. Would you mind if I call you next week?"

Or,

"I've really enjoyed your company. You're a fascinating conversationalist. I'd like to do this again. How about you?"

Now some final words about being a "kinder, gentler dater."

WE'LL DO LUNCH SOMETIME

Regardless of how your first meeting turns out, don't say that you will be in touch and then not do it. Make promises you intend to keep! If you find that special someone, let the others know so they aren't waiting by the phone for your call.

A simple statement will do, such as, "I've found someone special, and I won't be dating anyone else until I see how this relationship goes."

May was never the month of love, for May is full of flowers; But rather April, wet by kind, for love is full of showers.

Anonymous

CHAPTER THREE

RESPONDING TO THE PERSONALS

DEJA VU

"Select a publication, compose a response, make telephone calls, and then date."

Where have you read this before? (A clue: Chapter One, "The Ad.")

And what has that to do with responding to the personals? Whether you decide to place or respond to an ad, you'll find the overall process has much in common.

The major differences from responding to a personal ad and writing one are CONTROL AND MONEY.

CONTROL is on the up side. When you place the ad you are in complete control. You answer the responses that appeal to you and eliminate the ones that don't.

MONEY is on the down side. You have to pay for the ad.

However, using VOICE MAIL for personal ads can be free for the ad-placer.

VOICE MAIL

In some publications using Voice Mail the ad is free for the ad composer because the publication makes its money on the 900 number the respondents use for answering. In other publications you split the cost with your respondents - you pay for the ad (a nominal fee) - the respondents pay by the minute for their call. Voice Mail for personal ads is fully described in the "Introduction."

Voice Mail ads are great for busy people like my friend Kevin:

PUTTING VOICE MAIL TO WORK

Kevin, a single father, a skilled pianist, and a busy professional software marketing expert, was looking for a companion to have fun times with - someone who liked to share interests and friends, but more importantly someone who also was a caring person who liked the idea of being around a small child and being part of a family atmosphere.

Before responding to the "personals," Kevin had tried other ways of meeting women: the bar scene, single groups, and blind dates arranged by family and friends. Although he did meet many women, he was interested in finding just one, and he still hadn't met her.

THE "TARGETING SPECIFIED GROUPS" TECHNIQUE

Kevin's years of using marketing skills aided him in finding the perfect woman for him. Out there in the great sea of humanity, he knew the right woman was somewhere to be found. He also knew that it would be a numbers game. So he set out on his quest. His first consideration was to  select a local, "up-scale," young professional's business publication containing personal ads reflecting his lifestyle.

THE "KEY WORD" TECHNIQUE

He made a list of key words important to his lifestyle and then studied the selected publication's personals for a number of weeks before answering any ads. The key words for him were:

TALL BLONDE WITH BLUE EYES

Of course, it didn't hurt if the physical attributes were described as "tall, blonde, with blue eyes." But even if the women didn't match exactly, Kevin was willing to meet the ad placers...as long as some of the "key words" were there.

Kevin responded to 22 Voice Mail-type ads. All but one asked him to leave his phone number. The one exception left instructions - she wouldn't call back until her caller sent her a photograph accompanied by a letter describing himself.

Other men may have been put off by the request. However, Kevin, knowing he was involved in a numbers game, vowed to leave no stone unturned. Not only did he do as he was requested, he enclosed a tape of his music.

MARATHON DATING

Meanwhile, 19 of the 22 ad placers called back and wanted to meet him. The first three he took dining. He concluded from these encounters there was no need for long expensive dinner meetings. Now he realized he could trust his intuition: Armed with the ad information, plus one or two phone conversations, he would know in the first 10 minutes of face-to-face meetings whether there was any chemistry.

DOING HIS OWN THING

Accordingly, he scheduled meetings based around *customary lifestyle which included outings with his son: bicycle rides, playground activities, beach walks, and zoo visits.*

Love gives itself; it is not bought.

Henry Wadsworth Longfellow

ONE WOMAN MAN

Kevin, like so many people who date through the personal ads, began to realize he could have a date every night. However, since his goal was a relationship with only ONE particular woman, he began to consider placing a personal ad of his own.

Focusing exclusively on what he was seeking in a companion, the ad would include the following "key words":

> "Happy, well traveled, international, bright,
>
> tall, blonde with blue eyes."

"LIGHT MY FIRE"

Kevin didn't have to place an ad after all! The woman whom he had sent the letter, photo, and music tape turned out to be that SPECIAL   PERSON!

According to Kevin, "Not only is she all that I was searching for, we have a lot of chemistry going between us." (See the Introduction section, "The Rich And Famous Are Doing It," for the romantic story about Kevin and Karen.)

SO MANY MEN - SO MANY WOMEN - SO LITTLE TIME

Kevin used the personal ads in an EFFICIENT, EFFECTIVE, and PRACTICAL manner to find his dream woman. EFFICIENT because..... of his active family and work schedule, his search time for dating was limited. EFFECTIVE because..... he could target an area and market it. PRACTICAL because..... it was cost effective - a few phone calls and an occasional evening out. Yet, he knew..... that there were hundreds of women, perhaps thousands looking for a special man. All he had to do was see if he fit the description.

Likewise, the odds are in your favor a special person is searching for someone like you. But unlike a crap shoot, it's a numbers game until you two get together. Whether you are a man or woman, using the personal ads can work for you!

DECISIONS - DECISIONS

It's time to fine-tune what you want:

1. Decide your needs from a relationship. Lots of dates? A mate? A friend/companion? Do you wish to share common interests? Or do you just want to hang out with someone?

2. Select the publications that appeal to you. If you don't subscribe to periodicals, go to the public library. The resources for finding just the right type of personal ads for you are endless: Local newspapers, free weekly papers, magazines, newsletters.

Narrow down the selection process by asking yourself what activities would you love to enjoy with others? Airplanes? Art? Business? Camping? Magic? Music? RV traveling? Senior citizen activities?

Whatever your choice - don't be too generic! These days you don't have to be. Select the group you would like to share common interests with, then focus on your special interests. Let's say you feel comfortable around business people. Concentrate on individuals who have expertise in areas, such as: marketing, public relations, computers, or those who own their own businesses.

> We are shaped and fashioned by what we love.
>
> Johann Wolfgang von Goethe

KEY WORD TECHNIQUE

3.   Make a list of "key words" which are important to you, such as Kevin did:

        "Happy, well traveled, international, bright,
        tall, blonde with blue eyes."

4.   Read the personal ads watching for your "key words."

5.   Match your overall description with what they are looking for.

6.   Look for people who have basic physical characteristics you desire.

After you have read a great many personal ads, you will discover descriptive words sometimes take on a new meaning:

"Powerfully built, large, stocky, and husky" might mean an overweight man.

"Rubenesque, full-figured, full-hipped, queensize, plump, and buxom" could mean an overweight woman.

"Since physical characteristics can be cleverly hidden by stretching word usage, become familiar with some of the most significant "stretchings."

COMMON INTERESTS

7. Watch for common interests!: Fishing, boating, football, dancing, photography, tennis, etc.

8. Be on the alert for ads that have offensive overtones: "into contemporary but not contemptible music," or ...... "dislikes lazy, penniless, game players, bearded, overweight, sloppy alcoholics, drug users, or religious nuts" (all of these appeared in honest-to-goodness ads). It's okay for the ad placer to describe his or her likes and dislikes, but if you (as the reader) are offended, pass the ad by.

9. Consider the "MUSTS" in the ads:

    "Must like children."

    "Must not smoke" (usually written as N/S for nonsmoker).

    "Must be churchgoer" and so on.

    Usually with "musts" there are NO compromises, and with so many flexible people out there waiting to hear from you I'd pass the "musts" by - unless you are in agreement.

AUTHOR! AUTHOR!

It's time to respond! By now you have narrowed your choice to at least one ad. So here are some guidelines for you:

1. Stock up on a supply of stationery, greeting cards, and bond or computer paper - it doesn't matter. What is essential is to always use good taste in corresponding.

2. Cut out the ad that you have decided to respond to, and attach it to a piece of paper or 3" by 5" card (anything that you can take notes on). When you get a response from the advertiser, add any pertinent information to the card.

3. Word process, hand write, or type your response.   The means of getting the words on paper aren't important - what you put on paper is!

4.   Start your response by identifying something they wrote.

"Tennis bum wants to play singles."

The obvious response would be:

"Dear Tennis Bum," and so on .

15-LOVE

5.   Keep your response brief and to the point. Don't tell all you know. Be positive and upbeat. Compliment their ad:

"Dear Tennis Bum. Your ad was so intriguing I found myself wanting to play singles with you."

6.   Answer all requests in the ad as honestly as possible. If the advertiser likes tennis and you aren't a player, say so. Do say you'll learn (if you mean it.) Include information about yourself that relates to the ad.

To love is to be all made of sighs and tears.

William Shakespeare

7.   Mention your hobbies and special talents (gourmet cook, terrific dancer, or knowledgeable traveler).

8.   Send a photo if requested. Be creative! Have a friend shoot some pictures of you that relate to the ad. For instance, for the Tennis Bum shoot some pictures on the tennis court.

9.   Don't give out your address! Instead, give your first name and phone number. If you would rather they write than call, rent a P.O. box for your mail. Use whatever precautions make you feel secure. It may take a little longer getting together, but being relaxed will give you more confidence when you have your first meeting.

ANALYZE! REVIEW! EXPERIMENT! BUT NEVER GIVE UP UNTIL YOU FIND WHAT AND WHOM YOU WANT!

10.   Review the first two chapters ("The Ad," and "Filtering Your Responses"). This information, along with the material in this chapter and Chapter Four ("Tales of Love and Sex"), form a matrix providing a complete picture of getting together through the "personals."

It's time to move on to Chapter Four where you'll learn all about *sleazy ads, con artists, unusual ads, sex, and love.*

CHAPTER FOUR

TALES OF LOVE AND SEX

You have come to the end of this book, and you have followed the directions for placing an ad and/or responding to the "personals." You're busy dating, but you have a few questions in your mind. I'd like to know what they are, so please write to me, and I'll try to answer as time permits:

Baron Publications

P.O. Box 256

Laguna Beach, California 92651

Until I hear from you and can respond personally, I have prepared some questions others have asked me during my research.

Life is a flower of which love is the honey.

Victor Hugo

QUESTION: "While reading personal ads I have noticed some ads, whether subtle or blatant, suggesting sex-for-hire. Why do the publications printing these ads allow this?"

ANSWER: Years ago one of the reasons personal ads were looked upon negatively was because they were used by "Ladies of the Night" to make contact with men of means. These ads are still used for advertising sex-for-hire and are published, not only in sexually oriented publications, but in respectable papers (however, most publications screen thoroughly for this). Sometimes the men who answer these sexually-oriented ads find themselves in trouble.

On September 19, 1991, a headline of the *Los Angeles Times* read:

"STEAMY SEX TALE GETS EVEN
STEAMIER"

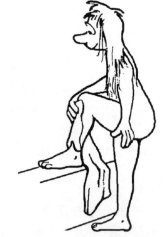

"Beautiful, young, frosted blonde seeking a generous, selective, successful executive for very discreet day/evening interludes."

That ad was placed by a Florida couple whose story is like no other hard-working prostitute and her protective pimp - the sensational story of a cop who says he suffers from spells of impotence and can't satisfy his wife, who claims she is a nymphomaniac. Allegedly, to cope with their sexual mismatch, the two say they established a $2,000-a-week brothel in their suburban home. She found the customers through the classifieds; he spied on her sexual encounters from their bedroom closet, and kept notes, and took videotapes.

Their flamboyant lawyer is making a novel argument that the voyeurism was central to the "therapy" with which the husband chose to save his marriage.

This wouldn't be the first time a man and wife teamed up to make a few bucks off the local citizenry. However, they allegedly kept careful records, including a list of about 50 "John Does" - some of whom have hired lawyers to keep the list out of the hands of the local media.

One name didn't stay out of the media: The Vice Mayor, a moral crusader who was so anti-vice he once persuaded the city to shut its nude bars. After it was leaked that his business card was found in the lady-in-question's bedroom, he resigned for "personal reasons."

This is a classic example of using the personal ads in a sexually oriented manner. My best advice is to read the ads carefully, and if you are uncomfortable with what is written, don't respond!.

QUESTION: "In your book you caution about some of the dangers associated with personal ads, but what other ways can the media be used to gain information about you?"

ANSWER: Long ago in England and France, the church, the nobility, and the common people were known as the three estates of the realm. Later, a fourth estate was added - the newspaper, because of its great influence upon public affairs. Newspaper power is greater than ever and with electronic technology, information can be disseminated into every home.

Unsavory people can read the news and find out all sorts of information about us that they can use for ill-gotten gain:

One example is an article that appeared in the *Daily Breeze*:

"CHARMER WITH THE LADIES ARRESTED ON FRAUD"

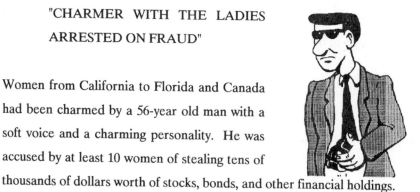

Women from California to Florida and Canada had been charmed by a 56-year old man with a soft voice and a charming personality. He was accused by at least 10 women of stealing tens of thousands of dollars worth of stocks, bonds, and other financial holdings.

According to the police, the "Charmer" was an average looking guy with a soft voice and a disarming personality.

In the Charmer's belongings detectives found stacks of clipped newspaper articles, a mixture of obituaries and stories detailing scams that men used to bilk women.

The Charmer's specialty was pursuing the widowed. He'd watch the obituaries for affluent men who had just passed away, leaving their wives rich widows. To get to their finances, he would prey on their emotions.

Personal ads can bring the unsavory like of gigolos, prostitutes, and con artists and their breed out of the woodwork.

Several letters I received had hints of gigolo in them, but one letter was more obvious:

> "Dear Beautiful Lady, I have blonde hair, blue eyes, am well built, and in much demand."

Again, read the personal ads carefully; the more SUBTLE the "come on," the more difficult it is to detect the writer's intention. The same goes for any responses you receive.

QUESTION: "I would like to place a personal ad, but I can't decide on which publication to use. Don't you think in my case I should go with a newspaper with a large circulation, even knowing the responses I receive will be generic?"

ANSWER: Although personal ads are published in many types of media, metropolitan newspapers proportionately publish the majority of them and have the widest circulation.

One paper in my area has a daily circulation of 1,000,000. Yearly, it runs thousands of personal ads. Since the editors stress they are not in the match-making business, you need to follow the rules for advertising acceptability in submitting personal ads:

- No names
- No personal addresses
- No phone numbers
- Use of good taste
- The first word must express a "common interest."

And since the newspaper alphabetizes ads, many people try to get theirs listed first by beginning the first word with *a*, *b*, or *c*. The first 17 ads I reviewed in last Sunday's edition started with the following words:

- Adventure (four of those)
- Adventurous
- Affectionate
- Arts and Music
- Bach to BBQ
- Beach/Romance
- Beach Walks
- Bike
- Buddhism
- Business
- Companionship
- Conversation
- Cooking
- Culture

In Chapter One, I described some of the pros and cons of placing an ad in a metropolitan newspaper. When you tell me you can't decide which publication to use, that signals to me you may not have focused on WHO YOU ARE AND WHAT YOU WANT. And to be successful with your ad in a major newspaper, you should stay focused, or you will get a mixture of responses. On the other hand sometimes that isn't all bad - it can help you in discovering who you are by exposing yourself to a variety of people....eventually leading you to write the "super ad" of your life!

If you haven't been able to select a publication that best represents you and the type of people you would like to meet, then perhaps the newspaper with the largest circulation in your area is the answer.

> There is no remedy for love but to love more.
>
> Henry Thoreau

QUESTION: "In the questionnaires in the book you stress compatibility, but when you first meet someone how do you know if you're alike, and why is it so important?"

ANSWER: The questionnaires emphasize helping you find out who you are and the qualities you would like in a partner.   In my observations of flourishing relationships, the couples who express similar traits and attitudes are likely to get along with each other harmoniously - enough to help them deal with the incompatibilities.

If you are having difficulty in determining the qualities you would like in a partner, possibly you haven't spent enough time finding out who you are.

Each of us unconsciously has a list of characteristics we want in a partner. When we are looking for a date/mate, we check out each new person we meet by matching our expectations to their traits and attitudes.

If you would be loved, love and be lovable.
Benjamin Franklin

Simply writing a reasonably good personal ad will enable you to make a conscious effort to identify the traits you possess and want in a mate/partner for a harmonious relationship. Completing the Ad Questionnaire (as described in Chapter One) is a way for you to find out what you really want in a mate/partner and what it will take to make you two compatible.

No matter how many lists of characteristics you make, it's possible your dream person doesn't exist. Be prepared to COMPROMISE. After all, you aren't perfect and he/she won't be either. But it will certainly give your relationship a better chance of surviving if you both have a few like qualities.

There will be things you may never wish to compromise - no matter how well the other traits match up. For example:

- Obligations to your children
- Financial situation and expectations
- Sexual expectations

KEEP YOUR GHOSTS IN THE CLOSET - DON'T TELL ALL YOU KNOW

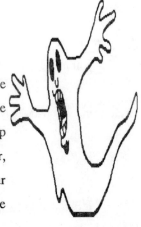

Some data about the other person is not always available to you at the outset of a relationship. And it shouldn't be disclosed at least until you can see where the relationship is going. Then, if it looks like you have a future together, you will need to discuss anything that may jeopardize your relationship. This should be done while you are in the courting stage, but LONG before the engagement.

FREE COMPATIBILITY PROBER

Once you have found that special person in your life, you may want to complete the What-If Compatibility Prober form (see Appendix, Form section), and submit it to Baron Publications for a free analysis.

The What-If Compatibility Prober is a tool that can give you a good idea, based upon long-tested and exhaustively researched principles, of how people with certain characteristics in their makeup are going to interact with you. You will learn whether two types of people can generally get along, or whether disputes and disagreements are practically "built in" to the relationship.

QUESTION: "After a long marriage, my wife and I divorced four years ago and I'm just back into the dating scene. I think of sex all the time, but I really don't know how many dates a couple should have before they enter into a sexual relationship."

ANSWER: In this day CASUAL SEX is dead, and AIDS awareness is chiefly responsible.

Studies show that men think about sex every two minutes - it probably isn't dimmed with AIDS awareness, but it certainly puts a damper on the good old days when a man could take sex wherever he found it.

As for women, experts report they think about sex once every 10 minutes.

Know your partner well before you have sexual intercourse. Even then, *insist* upon condoms or *abstain* from sexual intercourse until you both are sure you can't infect each other.

QUESTION: "How will I know when I'm in love? I'm not sure I'd know real love if it came up and bit me."

ANSWER: You aren't alone. Romance experts think that "What is this thing called love?" is one of the oldest questions since time immemorial. Poets have died over it, wars have been fought over it, fortunes have been gained or lost over it. Plato, 2400 years ago, pointed out that love is a form of madness.

The only satisfactory answer that I've been able to come up with is:

"Loving another person is wanting to insure their security, safety, well being and growth, and hopefully with some chemistry mixed in between."

OFFBEAT ADS

QUESTION: "In your years of research for this book, what was the most unusual ad?"

ANSWER: I have seen a great variety of ads - running the gamut from a lady who claimed to be a "Certified Country Girl," to a man who advertised himself as "34 and a Virgin." But the most curious ad was in the *Denver Post*:

"56 year WWM, President/CEO of Technological Corp. recently relocated to Denver, desires to establish interlocutory relationship with highly intelligent, imaginative personable, attractive and groomed woman-mid 30's to early 40's. I'm an aggressive, opinionated, demanding, egotistical male chauvinist example of the masculine species - totally capable of providing a secure and trouble-free financial and emotional environment for an ultra-feminine woman who prefers to cater to her feminine desires and intrinsic self-satisfaction, rather than compete in the professional marketplace."

"Acceptable candidate must be willing and capable of providing me with a serene non-competitive and non-aggressive personal environment and be instinctively and naturally sensuous, provocative, and uninhibited."

"I will respond **ONLY** to those replies that contain both full-length frontal and profile-definitive pictures and a descriptive letter outlining your desires and requirements and the personal criteria that you offer in return. All responses that do not meet my standards or criteria will be trashed. Candidates who meet or exceed my criteria will be contacted by telephone to arrange a meeting for mutual appraisal and evaluation of and by both parties. Address replies to: "PRESIDENT/CEO - PERSONAL"

Denver Post columnist, Kevin Simpson, interviewed the creator of the above ad to find out why an apparently successful businessman resorted to the classifieds for companionship.

The following is from Kevin's interview with the ad author when asked why he placed the ad.

"How are they going to know that I exist?" he retorts. "I'm not a social person. Last Friday night I went to some place down on Hampden, some meat market, and it was like a (censored) can of worms. Judas priest, it was a noisy madhouse. I'm 56 years old and that barroom environment isn't for me anymore."

TOO YOUNG - TOO DIFFERENT

Before he moved to Denver he ran a similar classified ad in a Des Moines paper. It triggered a torrent of protest and even an unflattering portrayal of him in a subsequent feature story on singles, but it also produced one caller who seemed to meet his criteria. Alas, she proved too young, too different. So this time he composed a more discriminating ad.

TELLING IT LIKE IT IS

"I rewrote it probably a dozen times," he says. "I can't be accused of putting up a false front or image. All my cards are on the table. Most people don't like that but to me, that's honesty. I look at it this way - I put in a pretty extensive advertisement, very explicit, to the point. There's no way a lady could read that ad and have the slightest misconception of what I'm looking for - unless she's stupid as hell, in which case I won't talk to her anyway."

He found true love once with an older woman. His marriage lasted three wonderful years before his wife died of cancer seven years ago. In the wake of his loss, he has surrendered to expediency. He won't hope for love again.

"I know inside of me I'm lonesome as hell since I lost her," he explains. "There's a hole in my life big as the (censored) Grand Canyon. So I look at this on a rational basis. The odds, statistically, against this lady answering my ad and falling in love are very minute. I don't expect it, so I won't be disappointed."

So it turns out that he is like so many of us. TOO BUSY TO TRY TO MEET PEOPLE THROUGH THE OLD WAYS: work, play, church, etc. But still hoping.....

AFTERWORD

No matter who, what, or where you are, there is a special someone out there waiting for you. Put your knowledge to work by:
- Following the step-by-step instructions.
- Using the "Key Word" technique.
- Completing "The Ad Questionnaire", "The Reponse Form", and "What If-Compatability Prober".

IT'S TIME!

You don't have to simply hope for chance encounters to find companionship and romance. Armed with the tools, you'll be able to create your ad quickly and with complete EASE!

SO, WRITE OR RESPOND TO AN AD

AND

NEVER BE LONELY AGAIN.

APPENDIX A

FORMS FOR YOU

1. The Ad Questionnaire

2. The Response Form

3. What If - Compatibility Prober

Using these forms will help you get results in your quest for fulfillment in your life.

1.   **The Ad Questionnaire,** Form 1000, quantity five - see Chapter One, "The Ad," - for instructions. This form is invaluable for putting together the right words for an exceptional personal ad. As you come to know the "Key Word" system you may want to revise your ad, so I have supplied you with five forms.

2.   **The Response Form,** Form 1001, quantity 18 - see Chapter Two, "Filtering Your Responses," - for instructions. This form is indispensable for keeping an efficient record of your responses.

3.   **What If - Compatibility Prober**, Form 1003, quantity one set - see Chapter Four, "Tales of Love and Sex." This form was developed by me to be used in conjunction with Dr. James H. Johnson's software program of the same name, and is an ingenious tool to match two personalities for compatibility. Quoting Dr. Johnson:

> "What If- Compatibility Prober is a tool that can give you a good idea, based upon long-tested and exhaustively researched principles, of how people with certain characteristics in their makeup are going to interact. You will learn whether two types of people can generally get along, or whether disputes and disagreements are practically 'built in' to the relationship."

> "Of course, there is no way of guaranteeing beyond the shadow of a doubt how a person will behave. What If - Compatibility Prober is a guideline, based on scientifically tested theory and supported by research, but there is always an element of unpredictability about every person. Everybody has some surprises in them."

When you find a "special person" have him/her complete Form 1003B, you complete Form 1003A, and mail both forms with a self-addressed, stamped envelope to Baron Publications for a free computer-generated report.

NOTE: Only original forms can be accepted. Do not send photocopies.

Two types of reports are available: a work place report and a personal relationships report. (Within the personal relationships report is a sexual fantasy report, but to receive it you must check the Sexual Fantasy box.)

The work place report begins with a broad overview of the dynamics and issues that can be expected in a relationship between two selected people. It is followed by an analysis of the relationship in each of several possible contexts: as co-workers, as worker to boss, and as boss to worker.

The personal relationships report also begins with a broad description of the relationship and then follows with sections covering platonic social interrelation. a love relationship from the male perspective, a love relationship from the female perspective, and the dynamics of managing your finances together.

To increase the accuracy of the report, it is important that you base your responses to various adjectives on their descriptions as shown on the form. These description are provided to take the guesswork out of the evaluation by explicitly expressing what Compatibility Prober means for each adjective.

Although the generation of the report is a free service for anyone buying this book, a data base is maintained. Therefore, if you meet someone new and wish to have that person analyzed: Send your request, a self-addressed stamped envelope, and ten dollars to Baron Publications. You will receive Form 1003B to be completed by the person you want analyzed.

THE AD QUESTIONNAIRE - STEP ONE
JUST WHO ARE YOU?

MARITAL STATUS:
(1) ☐ SINGLE   ☐ DIVORCED   ☐ WIDOW/WIDOWER

ETHNIC GROUP
(2)

SEX
(3) ☐ M ☐ F

VITAL STATISTICS:
(4)

AGE
a)

HEIGHT
b)

WEIGHT
c)

(5) DESCRIBE YOUR PHYSICAL AND MENTAL ATTRIBUTES IN FIVE WORDS OR LESS:

a) _____   d) _____

b) _____   e) _____

c) _____

(6) LIST, IN THE ORDER OF IMPORTANCE, HOBBIES AND SPORTS THAT YOU ENGAGE IN ON
A REGULAR BASIS.

a) HOBBIES _____

b) SPORTS _____

LIST THOSE THINGS THAT ARE "MUSTS" IN YOUR LIFE:
(7) _____

(8) PUT A CHECK MARK IN THE BOX THAT BEST DESCRIBES WHAT YOU'RE LOOKING FOR IN
A RELATIONSHIP:

a) ☐ MARRIAGE   b) ☐ ROMANCE   c) ☐ FRIENDSHIP

d) ☐ COMPANIONSHIP   e) ☐ COME-OUT-AND-PLAY   f) ☐ SOMETHING ELSE

(9) LIST THE FOUR MOST IMPORTANT QUALITIES YOU'RE LOOKING FOR IN THE PERSON YOU
WANT THE RELATIONSHIP WITH:

a) _____   c) _____

b) _____   d) _____

FORM 1000 (12-91)

THE AD QUESTIONNAIRE - STEP TWO
WHAT ARE YOU LOOKING FOR?

THERE MAY BE TYPES OF PEOPLE WHOM YOU WOULD PREFER TO DATE. MAKE A CHECK MARK OR FILL IN THE BLANK, AS APPLICABLE, IN THE APPROPRIATE BOX:

⑩ ETHNIC GROUP   a) ☐ CAUCASIAN   b) ☐ BLACK   c) ☐ HISPANIC
   I WILL DATE:

   d) ☐ ORIENTAL   e) ☐ DOES NOT MATTER   f) ☐ OTHER, _____

AGE RANGE I WILL DATE ⑪	⑫ HEIGHT RANGE I WILL DATE
⑬ DATING A SMOKER IS: ☐ OKAY ☐ NOT OKAY ☐ DOES NOT MATTER	⑭ DATING A SOCIAL DRINKER IS: ☐ OKAY ☐ NOT OKAY ☐ DOES NOT MATTER

THE AD QUESTIONNAIRE - STEP THREE
YOUR AD

⑮ _____

_____

_____

_____

_____

FORM 1000 (12-91) BACK

THE AD QUESTIONNAIRE - STEP ONE
JUST WHO ARE YOU?

MARITAL STATUS:

(1) ☐ SINGLE   ☐ DIVORCED   ☐ WIDOW/WIDOWER

ETHNIC GROUP (2)

SEX	VITAL STATISTICS:	AGE	HEIGHT	WEIGHT
(3) ☐ M ☐ F	(4)	a)	b)	c)

(5) DESCRIBE YOUR PHYSICAL AND MENTAL ATTRIBUTES IN FIVE WORDS OR LESS:

a) _____   d) _____

b) _____   e) _____

c) _____

(6) LIST, IN THE ORDER OF IMPORTANCE, HOBBIES AND SPORTS THAT YOU ENGAGE IN ON A REGULAR BASIS.

a) HOBBIES _____

b) SPORTS _____

LIST THOSE THINGS THAT ARE "MUSTS" IN YOUR LIFE:

(7) _____

(8) PUT A CHECK MARK IN THE BOX THAT BEST DESCRIBES WHAT YOU'RE LOOKING FOR IN A RELATIONSHIP:

a) ☐ MARRIAGE   b) ☐ ROMANCE   c) ☐ FRIENDSHIP

d) ☐ COMPANIONSHIP   e) ☐ COME-OUT-AND-PLAY   f) ☐ SOMETHING ELSE

(9) LIST THE FOUR MOST IMPORTANT QUALITIES YOU'RE LOOKING FOR IN THE PERSON YOU WANT THE RELATIONSHIP WITH:

a) _____   c) _____

b) _____   d) _____

FORM 1000 (12-91)

THE AD QUESTIONNAIRE - STEP TWO
WHAT ARE YOU LOOKING FOR?

THERE MAY BE TYPES OF PEOPLE WHOM YOU WOULD PREFER TO DATE. MAKE A CHECK MARK O
FILL IN THE BLANK, AS APPLICABLE, IN THE APPROPRIATE BOX:

(10) ETHNIC GROUP a) ☐ CAUCASIAN   b) ☐ BLACK   c) ☐ HISPANIC
I WILL DATE:

d) ☐ ORIENTAL   e) ☐ DOES NOT MATTER f) ☐ OTHER, _____

AGE RANGE I WILL DATE (11)	(12) HEIGHT RANGE I WILL DATE
(13) DATING A SMOKER IS:	(14) DATING A SOCIAL DRINKER IS:
☐ OKAY ☐ NOT OKAY ☐ DOES NOT MATTER	☐ OKAY ☐ NOT OKAY ☐ DOES NOT MATTE

THE AD QUESTIONNAIRE - STEP THREE
YOUR AD

(15) _____

_____

_____

_____

_____

FORM 1000 (12-91) BACK

THE AD QUESTIONNAIRE - STEP ONE
JUST WHO ARE YOU?

MARITAL STATUS:			ETHNIC GROUP

(1) ☐ SINGLE   ☐ DIVORCED   ☐ WIDOW/WIDOWER   (2)

SEX	VITAL STATISTICS:	AGE	HEIGHT	WEIGHT

(3) ☐ M ☐ F   (4)   a)   b)   c)

(5) DESCRIBE YOUR PHYSICAL AND MENTAL ATTRIBUTES IN FIVE WORDS OR LESS:

a) _____   d) _____

b) _____   e) _____

c) _____

(6) LIST, IN THE ORDER OF IMPORTANCE, HOBBIES AND SPORTS THAT YOU ENGAGE IN ON A REGULAR BASIS.

a) HOBBIES _____

b) SPORTS _____

LIST THOSE THINGS THAT ARE "MUSTS" IN YOUR LIFE:

(7) _____

(8) PUT A CHECK MARK IN THE BOX THAT BEST DESCRIBES WHAT YOU'RE LOOKING FOR IN A RELATIONSHIP:

a) ☐ MARRIAGE   b) ☐ ROMANCE   c) ☐ FRIENDSHIP

d) ☐ COMPANIONSHIP   e) ☐ COME-OUT-AND-PLAY   f) ☐ SOMETHING ELSE

(9) LIST THE FOUR MOST IMPORTANT QUALITIES YOU'RE LOOKING FOR IN THE PERSON YOU WANT THE RELATIONSHIP WITH:

a) _____   c) _____

b) _____   d) _____

FORM 1000 (12-91)

THE AD QUESTIONNAIRE - STEP TWO
WHAT ARE YOU LOOKING FOR?

THERE MAY BE TYPES OF PEOPLE WHOM YOU WOULD PREFER TO DATE. MAKE A CHECK MARK OF
FILL IN THE BLANK, AS APPLICABLE, IN THE APPROPRIATE BOX:

(10) ETHNIC GROUP a) ☐ CAUCASIAN   b) ☐ BLACK   c) ☐ HISPANIC
I WILL DATE:

d) ☐ ORIENTAL   e) ☐ DOES NOT MATTER   f) ☐ OTHER, _____

AGE RANGE I WILL DATE
(11)

(12) HEIGHT RANGE I WILL DATE

(13) DATING A SMOKER IS:

☐ OKAY   ☐ NOT OKAY   ☐ DOES NOT MATTER

(14) DATING A SOCIAL DRINKER IS:

☐ OKAY   ☐ NOT OKAY   ☐ DOES NOT MATTE

THE AD QUESTIONNAIRE - STEP THREE
YOUR AD

(15)

_____

_____

_____

_____

_____

FORM 1000 (12-91) BACK

THE AD QUESTIONNAIRE - STEP ONE
JUST WHO ARE YOU?

MARITAL STATUS:
(1) ☐ SINGLE ☐ DIVORCED ☐ WIDOW/WIDOWER

ETHNIC GROUP
(2)

SEX
(3) ☐ M ☐ F

VITAL STATISTICS:
(4)

AGE
a)

HEIGHT
b)

WEIGHT
c)

(5) DESCRIBE YOUR PHYSICAL AND MENTAL ATTRIBUTES IN FIVE WORDS OR LESS:

a) _____ d) _____

b) _____ e) _____

c) _____

(6) LIST, IN THE ORDER OF IMPORTANCE, HOBBIES AND SPORTS THAT YOU ENGAGE IN ON A REGULAR BASIS.

a) HOBBIES _____

b) SPORTS _____

LIST THOSE THINGS THAT ARE "MUSTS" IN YOUR LIFE:

(7) _____

(8) PUT A CHECK MARK IN THE BOX THAT BEST DESCRIBES WHAT YOU'RE LOOKING FOR IN A RELATIONSHIP:

a) ☐ MARRIAGE   b) ☐ ROMANCE   c) ☐ FRIENDSHIP

d) ☐ COMPANIONSHIP   e) ☐ COME-OUT-AND-PLAY   f) ☐ SOMETHING ELSE

(9) LIST THE FOUR MOST IMPORTANT QUALITIES YOU'RE LOOKING FOR IN THE PERSON YOU WANT THE RELATIONSHIP WITH:

a) _____ c) _____

b) _____ d) _____

FORM 1000 (12-91)

THE AD QUESTIONNAIRE - STEP TWO
WHAT ARE YOU LOOKING FOR?

THERE MAY BE TYPES OF PEOPLE WHOM YOU WOULD PREFER TO DATE. MAKE A CHECK MARK OR FILL IN THE BLANK, AS APPLICABLE, IN THE APPROPRIATE BOX:

(10) ETHNIC GROUP a) ☐ CAUCASIAN b) ☐ BLACK c) ☐ HISPANIC
    I WILL DATE:

    d) ☐ ORIENTAL e) ☐ DOES NOT MATTER f) ☐ OTHER, _____

AGE RANGE I WILL DATE (11)	HEIGHT RANGE I WILL DATE (12)
(13) DATING A SMOKER IS:	(14) DATING A SOCIAL DRINKER IS:
☐ OKAY ☐ NOT OKAY ☐ DOES NOT MATTER	☐ OKAY ☐ NOT OKAY ☐ DOES NOT MATTER

THE AD QUESTIONNAIRE - STEP THREE
YOUR AD

(15) _____

_____

_____

_____

_____

FORM 1000 (12-91) BACK

THE AD QUESTIONNAIRE - STEP ONE
JUST WHO ARE YOU?

MARITAL STATUS:				ETHNIC GROUP

(1) ☐ SINGLE   ☐ DIVORCED   ☐ WIDOW/WIDOWER   (2)

SEX	VITAL STATISTICS:	AGE	HEIGHT	WEIGHT
(3) ☐ M ☐ F	(4)	a)	b)	c)

(5) DESCRIBE YOUR PHYSICAL AND MENTAL ATTRIBUTES IN FIVE WORDS OR LESS:

a) _____   d) _____

b) _____   e) _____

c) _____

(6) LIST, IN THE ORDER OF IMPORTANCE, HOBBIES AND SPORTS THAT YOU ENGAGE IN ON A REGULAR BASIS.

a) HOBBIES _____

b) SPORTS _____

LIST THOSE THINGS THAT ARE "MUSTS" IN YOUR LIFE:

(7) _____

(8) PUT A CHECK MARK IN THE BOX THAT BEST DESCRIBES WHAT YOU'RE LOOKING FOR IN A RELATIONSHIP:

a) ☐ MARRIAGE   b) ☐ ROMANCE   c) ☐ FRIENDSHIP

d) ☐ COMPANIONSHIP   e) ☐ COME-OUT-AND-PLAY   f) ☐ SOMETHING ELSE

(9) LIST THE FOUR MOST IMPORTANT QUALITIES YOU'RE LOOKING FOR IN THE PERSON YOU WANT THE RELATIONSHIP WITH:

a) _____   c) _____

b) _____   d) _____

FORM 1000 (12-91)

THE AD QUESTIONNAIRE - STEP TWO
WHAT ARE YOU LOOKING FOR?

THERE MAY BE TYPES OF PEOPLE WHOM YOU WOULD PREFER TO DATE. MAKE A CHECK MARK OR FILL IN THE BLANK, AS APPLICABLE, IN THE APPROPRIATE BOX:

(10) ETHNIC GROUP a) ☐ CAUCASIAN   b) ☐ BLACK   c) ☐ HISPANIC
     I WILL DATE:

     d) ☐ ORIENTAL   e) ☐ DOES NOT MATTER   f) ☐ OTHER, _____

AGE RANGE I WILL DATE (11)	(12) HEIGHT RANGE I WILL DATE
(13) DATING A SMOKER IS:	(14) DATING A SOCIAL DRINKER IS:
☐ OKAY ☐ NOT OKAY ☐ DOES NOT MATTER	☐ OKAY ☐ NOT OKAY ☐ DOES NOT MATTER

THE AD QUESTIONNAIRE - STEP THREE
YOUR AD

(15) _____

_____

_____

_____

_____

FORM 1000 (12-91) BACK

THE RESPONSE FORM

LINE 1	ENVELOPE NO.	DATE RECEIVED

LINE 2	NOTE THE UNUSUAL

LINE 3	ENTER NAME	ADDRESS

LINE 4	TEL. NO.	AGE	HEIGHT	WEIGHT

LINE 5	OTHER INFORMATION

LINE 6	CULTURAL INTERESTS: THEATRE	DANCE	MUSIC	VISUAL ARTS	FILM

LINE 7	MARITAL STATUS: NEVER MARRIED	DIVORCED	WIDOW/WIDOWER

LINE 8	CHILDREN: HAS	HASN'T	DESIRES	NO OPINION

LINE 9	RELIGION: PROTESTANT	CATHOLIC	JEWISH	AGNOSTIC	ATHEIST	OTHER

LINE 10	RATING: EXCELLENT	GOOD	FORGET IT

NOTES:

FORM 1001 (12-91)

THE RESPONSE FORM

LINE 1	ENVELOPE NO. DATE RECEIVED
LINE 2	NOTE THE UNUSUAL
LINE 3	ENTER NAME ADDRESS
LINE 4	TEL. NO. AGE HEIGHT WEIGHT
LINE 5	OTHER INFORMATION
LINE 6	CULTURAL INTERESTS: THEATRE DANCE MUSIC VISUAL ARTS FILM
LINE 7	MARITAL STATUS: NEVER MARRIED DIVORCED WIDOW/WIDOWER
LINE 8	CHILDREN: HAS HASN'T DESIRES NO OPINION
LINE 9	RELIGION: PROTESTANT CATHOLIC JEWISH AGNOSTIC ATHEIST OTHER
LINE 10	RATING: EXCELLENT GOOD FORGET IT

NOTES:

_____

_____

_____

_____

THE RESPONSE FORM

LINE 1	ENVELOPE NO.	DATE RECEIVED

LINE 2	NOTE THE UNUSUAL

LINE 3	ENTER NAME	ADDRESS

LINE 4	TEL. NO.	AGE	HEIGHT	WEIGHT

LINE 5	OTHER INFORMATION

LINE 6	CULTURAL INTERESTS: THEATRE	DANCE	MUSIC	VISUAL ARTS	FILM

LINE 7	MARITAL STATUS: NEVER MARRIED	DIVORCED	WIDOW/WIDOWER

LINE 8	CHILDREN: HAS	HASN'T	DESIRES	NO OPINION

LINE 9	RELIGION: PROTESTANT	CATHOLIC	JEWISH	AGNOSTIC	ATHEIST	OTHER

LINE 10	RATING: EXCELLENT	GOOD	FORGET IT

NOTES:

_____

_____

_____

_____

_____

FORM 1001 (12-91)

THE RESPONSE FORM

LINE 1	ENVELOPE NO.	DATE RECEIVED
LINE 2	NOTE THE UNUSUAL	
LINE 3	ENTER NAME	ADDRESS

LINE 4	TEL. NO.	AGE	HEIGHT	WEIGHT

LINE 5	OTHER INFORMATION

LINE 6	CULTURAL INTERESTS: THEATRE	DANCE	MUSIC	VISUAL ARTS	FILM
LINE 7	MARITAL STATUS: NEVER MARRIED	DIVORCED		WIDOW/WIDOWER	
LINE 8	CHILDREN: HAS	HASN'T	DESIRES	NO OPINION	
LINE 9	RELIGION: PROTESTANT	CATHOLIC	JEWISH	AGNOSTIC	ATHEIST	OTHER
LINE 10	RATING: EXCELLENT	GOOD	FORGET IT		

NOTES:

_____

_____

_____

_____

FORM 1001 (12-91)

THE RESPONSE FORM

LINE 1	ENVELOPE NO.		DATE RECEIVED	

LINE 2 — NOTE THE UNUSUAL

LINE 3	ENTER NAME	ADDRESS		

LINE 4	TEL. NO.	AGE	HEIGHT	WEIGHT

LINE 5 — OTHER INFORMATION

LINE 6	CULTURAL INTERESTS: THEATRE	DANCE	MUSIC	VISUAL ARTS	FILM

LINE 7	MARITAL STATUS: NEVER MARRIED	DIVORCED	WIDOW/WIDOWER

LINE 8	CHILDREN: HAS	HASN'T	DESIRES	NO OPINION

LINE 9	RELIGION: PROTESTANT	CATHOLIC	JEWISH	AGNOSTIC	ATHEIST	OTHER

LINE 10	RATING: EXCELLENT	GOOD	FORGET IT

NOTES:

FORM 1001 (12-91)

THE RESPONSE FORM

LINE 1	ENVELOPE NO.	DATE RECEIVED

LINE 2	NOTE THE UNUSUAL

LINE 3	ENTER NAME	ADDRESS

LINE 4	TEL. NO.	AGE	HEIGHT	WEIGHT

LINE 5	OTHER INFORMATION

LINE 6	CULTURAL INTERESTS: THEATRE	DANCE	MUSIC	VISUAL ARTS	FILM

LINE 7	MARITAL STATUS: NEVER MARRIED	DIVORCED	WIDOW/WIDOWER

LINE 8	CHILDREN: HAS	HASN'T	DESIRES	NO OPINION

LINE 9	RELIGION: PROTESTANT	CATHOLIC	JEWISH	AGNOSTIC	ATHEIST	OTHER

LINE 10	RATING: EXCELLENT	GOOD	FORGET IT

NOTES:

_____

_____

_____

_____

FORM 1001 (12-91)

THE RESPONSE FORM

LINE 1	ENVELOPE NO. / DATE RECEIVED

LINE 2	NOTE THE UNUSUAL

LINE 3	ENTER NAME / ADDRESS

LINE 4	TEL. NO. / AGE / HEIGHT / WEIGHT

LINE 5	OTHER INFORMATION

LINE 6	CULTURAL INTERESTS: THEATRE / DANCE / MUSIC / VISUAL ARTS / FILM

LINE 7	MARITAL STATUS: NEVER MARRIED / DIVORCED / WIDOW/WIDOWER

LINE 8	CHILDREN: HAS / HASN'T / DESIRES / NO OPINION

LINE 9	RELIGION: PROTESTANT / CATHOLIC / JEWISH / AGNOSTIC / ATHEIST / OTHER

LINE 10	RATING: EXCELLENT / GOOD / FORGET IT

NOTES:

_____

_____

_____

_____

THE RESPONSE FORM

LINE 1	ENVELOPE NO. / DATE RECEIVED
LINE 2	NOTE THE UNUSUAL
LINE 3	ENTER NAME / ADDRESS
LINE 4	TEL. NO. / AGE / HEIGHT / WEIGHT
LINE 5	OTHER INFORMATION
LINE 6	CULTURAL INTERESTS: THEATRE / DANCE / MUSIC / VISUAL ARTS / FILM
LINE 7	MARITAL STATUS: NEVER MARRIED / DIVORCED / WIDOW/WIDOWER
LINE 8	CHILDREN: HAS / HASN'T / DESIRES / NO OPINION
LINE 9	RELIGION: PROTESTANT / CATHOLIC / JEWISH / AGNOSTIC / ATHEIST / OTHER
LINE 10	RATING: EXCELLENT / GOOD / FORGET IT

NOTES:

_____

_____

_____

_____

FORM 1001 (12-91)

THE RESPONSE FORM

LINE 1	ENVELOPE NO. / DATE RECEIVED
LINE 2	NOTE THE UNUSUAL
LINE 3	ENTER NAME / ADDRESS
LINE 4	TEL. NO. / AGE / HEIGHT / WEIGHT
LINE 5	OTHER INFORMATION
LINE 6	CULTURAL INTERESTS: THEATRE / DANCE / MUSIC / VISUAL ARTS / FILM
LINE 7	MARITAL STATUS: NEVER MARRIED / DIVORCED / WIDOW/WIDOWER
LINE 8	CHILDREN: HAS / HASN'T / DESIRES / NO OPINION
LINE 9	RELIGION: PROTESTANT / CATHOLIC / JEWISH / AGNOSTIC / ATHEIST / OTHER
LINE 10	RATING: EXCELLENT / GOOD / FORGET IT

NOTES:

_____

_____

_____

_____

FORM 1001 (12-91)

THE RESPONSE FORM

LINE 1	ENVELOPE NO.	DATE RECEIVED

LINE 1 — ENVELOPE NO. / DATE RECEIVED

LINE 2 — NOTE THE UNUSUAL

LINE 3 — ENTER NAME / ADDRESS

LINE 4 — TEL. NO. / AGE / HEIGHT / WEIGHT

LINE 5 — OTHER INFORMATION

LINE 6 — CULTURAL INTERESTS: THEATRE / DANCE / MUSIC / VISUAL ARTS / FILM

LINE 7 — MARITAL STATUS: NEVER MARRIED / DIVORCED / WIDOW/WIDOWER

LINE 8 — CHILDREN: HAS / HASN'T / DESIRES / NO OPINION

LINE 9 — RELIGION: PROTESTANT / CATHOLIC / JEWISH / AGNOSTIC / ATHEIST / OTHER

LINE 10 — RATING: EXCELLENT / GOOD / FORGET IT

NOTES:

THE RESPONSE FORM

LINE 1	ENVELOPE NO.		DATE RECEIVED	

LINE 2	NOTE THE UNUSUAL

LINE 3	ENTER NAME	ADDRESS

LINE 4	TEL. NO.	AGE	HEIGHT	WEIGHT

LINE 5	OTHER INFORMATION

LINE 6	CULTURAL INTERESTS: THEATRE	DANCE	MUSIC	VISUAL ARTS	FILM

LINE 7	MARITAL STATUS: NEVER MARRIED	DIVORCED	WIDOW/WIDOWER

LINE 8	CHILDREN: HAS	HASN'T	DESIRES	NO OPINION

LINE 9	RELIGION: PROTESTANT	CATHOLIC	JEWISH	AGNOSTIC	ATHEIST	OTHER

LINE 10	RATING: EXCELLENT	GOOD	FORGET IT

NOTES:

_____

_____

_____

_____

FORM 1001 (12-91)

THE RESPONSE FORM

LINE 1	ENVELOPE NO. / DATE RECEIVED
LINE 2	NOTE THE UNUSUAL
LINE 3	ENTER NAME / ADDRESS
LINE 4	TEL. NO. / AGE / HEIGHT / WEIGHT
LINE 5	OTHER INFORMATION
LINE 6	CULTURAL INTERESTS: THEATRE / DANCE / MUSIC / VISUAL ARTS / FILM
LINE 7	MARITAL STATUS: NEVER MARRIED / DIVORCED / WIDOW/WIDOWER
LINE 8	CHILDREN: HAS / HASN'T / DESIRES / NO OPINION
LINE 9	RELIGION: PROTESTANT / CATHOLIC / JEWISH / AGNOSTIC / ATHEIST / OTHER
LINE 10	RATING: EXCELLENT / GOOD / FORGET IT

NOTES:

_____

_____

_____

_____

FORM 1001 (12-91)

THE RESPONSE FORM

LINE 1	ENVELOPE NO.	DATE RECEIVED

LINE 2	NOTE THE UNUSUAL

LINE 3	ENTER NAME	ADDRESS

LINE 4	TEL. NO.	AGE	HEIGHT	WEIGHT

LINE 5	OTHER INFORMATION

LINE 6	CULTURAL INTERESTS: THEATRE	DANCE	MUSIC	VISUAL ARTS	FILM

LINE 7	MARITAL STATUS: NEVER MARRIED	DIVORCED	WIDOW/WIDOWER

LINE 8	CHILDREN: HAS	HASN'T	DESIRES	NO OPINION

LINE 9	RELIGION: PROTESTANT	CATHOLIC	JEWISH	AGNOSTIC	ATHEIST	OTHER

LINE 10	RATING: EXCELLENT	GOOD	FORGET IT

NOTES:

_____

_____

_____

_____

THE RESPONSE FORM

LINE 1	ENVELOPE NO.	DATE RECEIVED

LINE 2	NOTE THE UNUSUAL

LINE 3	ENTER NAME	ADDRESS

LINE 4	TEL. NO.	AGE	HEIGHT	WEIGHT

LINE 5	OTHER INFORMATION

LINE 6	CULTURAL INTERESTS: THEATRE	DANCE	MUSIC	VISUAL ARTS	FILM

LINE 7	MARITAL STATUS: NEVER MARRIED	DIVORCED	WIDOW/WIDOWER

LINE 8	CHILDREN: HAS	HASN'T	DESIRES	NO OPINION

LINE 9	RELIGION: PROTESTANT	CATHOLIC	JEWISH	AGNOSTIC	ATHEIST	OTHER

LINE 10	RATING: EXCELLENT	GOOD	FORGET IT

NOTES:

_____

_____

_____

_____

THE RESPONSE FORM

LINE 1	ENVELOPE NO.	DATE RECEIVED
LINE 2	NOTE THE UNUSUAL	
LINE 3	ENTER NAME	ADDRESS

LINE 4	TEL. NO.	AGE	HEIGHT	WEIGHT

LINE 5	OTHER INFORMATION

LINE 6	CULTURAL INTERESTS: THEATRE	DANCE	MUSIC	VISUAL ARTS	FILM

LINE 7	MARITAL STATUS: NEVER MARRIED	DIVORCED	WIDOW/WIDOWER

LINE 8	CHILDREN: HAS	HASN'T	DESIRES	NO OPINION

LINE 9	RELIGION: PROTESTANT	CATHOLIC	JEWISH	AGNOSTIC	ATHEIST	OTHER

LINE 10	RATING: EXCELLENT	GOOD	FORGET IT

NOTES:

THE RESPONSE FORM

LINE 1	ENVELOPE NO.	DATE RECEIVED

LINE 2	NOTE THE UNUSUAL

LINE 3	ENTER NAME	ADDRESS

LINE 4	TEL. NO.	AGE	HEIGHT	WEIGHT

LINE 5	OTHER INFORMATION

LINE 6	CULTURAL INTERESTS: THEATRE	DANCE	MUSIC	VISUAL ARTS	FILM

LINE 7	MARITAL STATUS: NEVER MARRIED	DIVORCED	WIDOW/WIDOWER

LINE 8	CHILDREN: HAS	HASN'T	DESIRES	NO OPINION

LINE 9	RELIGION: PROTESTANT	CATHOLIC	JEWISH	AGNOSTIC	ATHEIST	OTHER

LINE 10	RATING: EXCELLENT	GOOD	FORGET IT

NOTES:

_____

_____

_____

_____

FORM 1001 (12-91)

THE RESPONSE FORM

LINE 1	ENVELOPE NO.		DATE RECEIVED	
LINE 2	NOTE THE UNUSUAL			
LINE 3	ENTER NAME	ADDRESS		
LINE 4	TEL. NO.	AGE	HEIGHT	WEIGHT
LINE 5	OTHER INFORMATION			
LINE 6	CULTURAL INTERESTS: THEATRE	DANCE	MUSIC	VISUAL ARTS	FILM
LINE 7	MARITAL STATUS: NEVER MARRIED	DIVORCED	WIDOW/WIDOWER	
LINE 8	CHILDREN: HAS	HASN'T	DESIRES	NO OPINION
LINE 9	RELIGION: PROTESTANT	CATHOLIC	JEWISH	AGNOSTIC	ATHEIST	OTHER
LINE 10	RATING: EXCELLENT	GOOD	FORGET IT	

NOTES:

THE RESPONSE FORM

LINE 1	ENVELOPE NO.		DATE RECEIVED		

LINE 2 — NOTE THE UNUSUAL

LINE 3	ENTER NAME	ADDRESS		

LINE 4	TEL. NO.	AGE	HEIGHT	WEIGHT

LINE 5 — OTHER INFORMATION

LINE 6	CULTURAL INTERESTS: THEATRE	DANCE	MUSIC	VISUAL ARTS	FILM

LINE 7	MARITAL STATUS: NEVER MARRIED	DIVORCED	WIDOW/WIDOWER

LINE 8	CHILDREN: HAS	HASN'T	DESIRES	NO OPINION

LINE 9	RELIGION: PROTESTANT	CATHOLIC	JEWISH	AGNOSTIC	ATHEIST	OTHER

LINE 10	RATING: EXCELLENT	GOOD	FORGET IT

NOTES:

_____

_____

_____

_____

WHAT IF - COMPATIBILITY PROBER
NEURALYTIC SYSTEMS

Check the appropriate box below for the type of report you want. If you want all three reports, check all three boxes.

☐ PERSONAL RELATIONSHIPS REPORT   ☐ WORKPLACE REPORT

☐ SEXUAL FANTASY REPORT

FIRST NAME (PRINT)		LAST NAME (PRINT)	
AGE	SEX	MARRIED ☐ YES ☐ NO	YEARS OF SCHOOL

Select one of the four possible responses following each adjective (trait). There are 48 adjectives and all 48 must be addressed. The responses range from strong agreement to strong disagreement.

ADJECTIVE	AGREE	MILDLY AGREE	MILDLY DISAGREE	DISAGREE
ACHIEVING - Known for succeeding.	☐	☐	☐	☐
AGGRESSIVE - Full of enterprise and initiative; bold and assertive.	☐	☐	☐	☐
AMBITIOUS - Works hard to achieve.	☐	☐	☐	☐
ARGUMENTATIVE - Easily disagrees or quarrels with others.	☐	☐	☐	☐
ANXIOUS - Often apprehensive or worried.	☐	☐	☐	☐
BRILLIANT - Someone with extremely high IQ.	☐	☐	☐	☐
CHEERFUL - Having a sunny disposition.	☐	☐	☐	☐
COMPULSIVE - Worries excessively about small details.	☐	☐	☐	☐
CONSCIENTIOUS - Concerned about doing things right.	☐	☐	☐	☐
CONSERVATIVE - Tends to be moderate and cautious.	☐	☐	☐	☐
DIPLOMATIC - Tactful in relations with other people.	☐	☐	☐	☐
DOMINANT - Controls or takes charge of others.	☐	☐	☐	☐

WHAT IF - COMPATIBILITY PROBER
NEURALYTIC SYSTEMS

FIRST NAME (PRINT)	LAST NAME (PRINT)

ADJECTIVE	AGREE	MILDLY AGREE	MILDLY DISAGREE	DISAGREE
DRIVEN - Strong and apparent internal motivation to succeed.	☐	☐	☐	☐
EASY GOING - Good natured; not often perturbed.	☐	☐	☐	☐
EMOTIONAL - Easily aroused to emotion.	☐	☐	☐	☐
EXCITABLE - Easily worried or upset; tense.	☐	☐	☐	☐
FRIENDLY - Likeable and good natured.	☐	☐	☐	☐
HARD-HEADED - Refuses to yield or comply; stubborn.	☐	☐	☐	☐
HARD-WORKING - Puts in long hours on projects; dedicated.	☐	☐	☐	☐
HEAD-STRONG - Determined to do as one pleases.	☐	☐	☐	☐
HIGH-STRUNG - Easily knocked off balance by even minor events.	☐	☐	☐	☐
HIGHLY EDUCATED - More literate and degreed than most.	☐	☐	☐	☐
HONEST - Truthful and trustworthy; fair.	☐	☐	☐	☐
HUMOROUS - Funny, amusing and outgoing.	☐	☐	☐	☐
IMAGINATIVE - Creative, inventive, and original.	☐	☐	☐	☐
INDEPENDENT - Self-determined and self-reliant.	☐	☐	☐	☐

FORM 1003A (12-91) BACK

WHAT IF - COMPATIBILITY PROBER
NEURALYTIC SYSTEMS

FIRST NAME (PRINT)	LAST NAME (PRINT)

ADJECTIVE	AGREE	MILDLY AGREE	MILDLY DISAGREE	DISAGREE
INTELLIGENT - Learns and understands better than most.	☐	☐	☐	☐
KNOWLEDGEABLE - Fluent in many subjects and areas.	☐	☐	☐	☐
MOODY - Gloomy and unpredictable.	☐	☐	☐	☐
NERVOUS - Emotionally tense.	☐	☐	☐	☐
OPINIONATED - Holds strong opinions on everything.	☐	☐	☐	☐
OPTIMISTIC - Usually takes the most hopeful, cheerful view.	☐	☐	☐	☐
ORDERLY - Neat and original.	☐	☐	☐	☐
OUTGOING - Extroverted and social.	☐	☐	☐	☐
PESSIMISTIC - Usually takes the worst, gloomiest view possible.	☐	☐	☐	☐
PREOCCUPIED - Frequently engrossed in own thoughts.	☐	☐	☐	☐
RELIABLE - Can be counted on.	☐	☐	☐	☐
SMART - Quick to figure things out.	☐	☐	☐	☐
SOCIABLE - More outgoing and people-minded than most.	☐	☐	☐	☐
STUBBORN - Obstinate and unyielding.	☐	☐	☐	☐

WHAT IF - COMPATIBILITY PROBER
NEURALYTIC SYSTEMS

FIRST NAME (PRINT)	LAST NAME (PRINT)

ADJECTIVE	AGREE	MILDLY AGREE	MILDLY DISAGREE	DISAGREE
SUCCESS ORIENTED - More concerned about success than most.	☐	☐	☐	☐
TALKATIVE - Talks more than most.	☐	☐	☐	☐
TEMPERAMENTAL - Having a moody nature; easily upset.	☐	☐	☐	☐
TENSE - Easily feels stress or anxiety.	☐	☐	☐	☐
THRILL-SEEKING - Craving excitement and change.	☐	☐	☐	☐
TOUGH-MINDED - Looks at all things logically, disregarding effect on people.	☐	☐	☐	☐
VERSATILE - Competent in many things.	☐	☐	☐	☐
WORRYING - Worries more than most.	☐	☐	☐	☐

When you have completed Form A and the person you want analyzed has completed Form B, mail them with a self-addressed stamped envelope to:

BARON PUBLICATIONS
P.O. BOX 256
LAGUNA BEACH, CA 92651

FORM 1003A (12-91) BACK

WHAT IF - COMPATIBILITY PROBER
NEURALYTIC SYSTEMS

Check the appropriate box below for the type of report you want. If you want all three reports, check all three boxes.

☐ PERSONAL RELATIONSHIPS REPORT ☐ WORKPLACE REPORT

☐ SEXUAL FANTASY REPORT

FIRST NAME (PRINT)		LAST NAME (PRINT)	
AGE	SEX	MARRIED ☐ YES ☐ NO	YEARS OF SCHOOL

Select one of the four possible responses following each adjective (trait). There are 48 adjectives and all 48 must be addressed. The responses range from strong agreement to strong disagreement.

ADJECTIVE	AGREE	MILDLY AGREE	MILDLY DISAGREE	DISAGREE
ACHIEVING - Known for succeeding.	☐	☐	☐	☐
AGGRESSIVE - Full of enterprise and initiative; bold and assertive.	☐	☐	☐	☐
AMBITIOUS - Works hard to achieve.	☐	☐	☐	☐
ARGUMENTATIVE - Easily disagrees or quarrels with others.	☐	☐	☐	☐
ANXIOUS - Often apprehensive or worried.	☐	☐	☐	☐
BRILLIANT - Someone with extremely high IQ.	☐	☐	☐	☐
CHEERFUL - Having a sunny disposition.	☐	☐	☐	☐
COMPULSIVE - Worries excessively about small details.	☐	☐	☐	☐
CONSCIENTIOUS - Concerned about doing things right.	☐	☐	☐	☐
CONSERVATIVE - Tends to be moderate and cautious.	☐	☐	☐	☐
DIPLOMATIC - Tactful in relations with other people.	☐	☐	☐	☐
DOMINANT - Controls or takes charge of others.	☐	☐	☐	☐

FORM 1003B (12-91)

WHAT IF - COMPATIBILITY PROBER
NEURALYTIC SYSTEMS

FIRST NAME (PRINT)	LAST NAME (PRINT)

ADJECTIVE	AGREE	MILDLY AGREE	MILDLY DISAGREE	DISAGREE
DRIVEN - Strong and apparent internal motivation to succeed.	☐	☐	☐	☐
EASY GOING - Good natured; not often perturbed.	☐	☐	☐	☐
EMOTIONAL - Easily aroused to emotion.	☐	☐	☐	☐
EXCITABLE - Easily worried or upset; tense.	☐	☐	☐	☐
FRIENDLY - Likeable and good natured.	☐	☐	☐	☐
HARD-HEADED - Refuses to yield or comply; stubborn.	☐	☐	☐	☐
HARD-WORKING - Puts in long hours on projects; dedicated.	☐	☐	☐	☐
HEAD-STRONG - Determined to do as one pleases.	☐	☐	☐	☐
HIGH-STRUNG - Easily knocked off balance by even minor events.	☐	☐	☐	☐
HIGHLY EDUCATED - More literate and degreed than most.	☐	☐	☐	☐
HONEST - Truthful and trustworthy; fair.	☐	☐	☐	☐
HUMOROUS - Funny, amusing and outgoing.	☐	☐	☐	☐
IMAGINATIVE - Creative, inventive, and original.	☐	☐	☐	☐
INDEPENDENT - Self-determined and self-reliant.	☐	☐	☐	☐

WHAT IF - COMPATIBILITY PROBER
NEURALYTIC SYSTEMS

FIRST NAME (PRINT)	LAST NAME (PRINT)

ADJECTIVE	AGREE	MILDLY AGREE	MILDLY DISAGREE	DISAGREE
INTELLIGENT - Learns and understands better than most.	☐	☐	☐	☐
KNOWLEDGEABLE - Fluent in many subjects and areas.	☐	☐	☐	☐
MOODY - Gloomy and unpredictable.	☐	☐	☐	☐
NERVOUS - Emotionally tense.	☐	☐	☐	☐
OPINIONATED - Holds strong opinions on everything.	☐	☐	☐	☐
OPTIMISTIC - Usually takes the most hopeful, cheerful view.	☐	☐	☐	☐
ORDERLY - Neat and original.	☐	☐	☐	☐
OUTGOING - Extroverted and social.	☐	☐	☐	☐
PESSIMISTIC - Usually takes the worst, gloomiest view possible.	☐	☐	☐	☐
PREOCCUPIED - Frequently engrossed in own thoughts.	☐	☐	☐	☐
RELIABLE - Can be counted on.	☐	☐	☐	☐
SMART - Quick to figure things out.	☐	☐	☐	☐
SOCIABLE - More outgoing and people-minded than most.	☐	☐	☐	☐
STUBBORN - Obstinate and unyielding.	☐	☐	☐	☐

WHAT IF - COMPATIBILITY PROBER
NEURALYTIC SYSTEMS

FIRST NAME (PRINT)	LAST NAME (PRINT)

ADJECTIVE	AGREE	MILDLY AGREE	MILDLY DISAGREE	DISAGREE
SUCCESS ORIENTED - More concerned about success than most.	☐	☐	☐	☐
TALKATIVE - Talks more than most.	☐	☐	☐	☐
TEMPERAMENTAL - Having a moody nature; easily upset.	☐	☐	☐	☐
TENSE - Easily feels stress or anxiety.	☐	☐	☐	☐
THRILL-SEEKING - Craving excitement and change.	☐	☐	☐	☐
TOUGH-MINDED - Looks at all things logically, disregarding effect on people.	☐	☐	☐	☐
VERSATILE - Competent in many things.	☐	☐	☐	☐
WORRYING - Worries more than most.	☐	☐	☐	☐

When you have completed Form A and the person you want analyzed has completed Form B, mail them with a self-addressed stamped envelope to:

BARON PUBLICATIONS
P.O. BOX 256
LAGUNA BEACH, CA 92651

APPENDIX B

GLOSSARY

MOST COMMONLY USED ACRONYMS/ABBREVIATIONS

Use acronym/abbreviation (coded words) when the publication that you select charges by the line rather than a flat fee for the ad. This allows you to get more into your ad for less money.

Use Appendix B in conjunction with the Ad Questionnaire (see Chapter One, "The Ad").

When reading personal ads many people do a cursory review by reading the first couple words. Those words are what will get them to read your entire ad.

SHOW STOPPERS

Starting your ad with at least one show stopper (catchy adjective) will give your ad an edge over other ads. The Voice Mail ads are generally free to you, and you may be allowed to put catchy little phrases printed in bold to lead off your ad. Here are a few eye-catchers:

QUOTED FROM THE MALE POINT OF VIEW

"DEEP DOWN I'M SHALLOW,"..... "DANCES WITH FOXES,"..... "DANCES WITH CHICKENS,"..... "SOON TO BE $$$,"..... "VALUABLE GENES,"..... "I'M SO SUAVE I COULD BARF."

QUOTED FROM THE FEMALE POINT OF VIEW

"MARGARITAVILLE,"..... "PETITE AND SPUNKY,"..... "FORMER BEAUTY QUEEN,"..... "FOR YOUR TOMORROWS,"..... "DO YOU BELIEVE?"..... "BEAUTY AND BRAINS."

Generally, the abbreviations for the basic statistics are somewhere near the beginning of the ad: marital status, race, and sex.
For example:

S/W/F = Single White Female or for S/W/M = Single White Male
S/B/F = Single Black Female or S/B/M = Single Black Male
S/J/F = could be Single Jewish Female or Single Japanese Female

S	= Single	W	= White	F	= Female
D	= Divorced	B	= Black	M	= Male
W	= Widow/Widower	H	= Hispanic		
NM	= Never Married	L	= Latino		
M	= Married	A	= Asian		
G	= Gay	O	= Oriental		
Bi	= Bisexual	J	= Jewish		
		J	= Japanese		
		NA	= Native American		

MISCELLANOUS

TFTG	= Too Far To Go
UL	= Undesirable Location
LTR	= Long Term Relationship
Fin. Sec.	= Financially Secure
N/S	= Non-Smoker
N/D	= Non-Drinker
P/P	= Phone/Photo
HW/LTR	= Hand-Written Letter
Adr	= Address
Sks	= Seeks
Slfemplyd	= Self-employed
Profl	= Professional
Trvl	= Travel
NSJMFNYC	= Nice Single Jewish Male From New York City

SUPERIOR WORDS TO DESCRIBE YOU/THEM

HEIGHT

Short, slight, small, diminutive.

Tall, large, long, rambling

WEIGHT/PHYSIQUE/FIGURE

FOR MEN

Muscular, athletic, powerfully built, solid.

FOR WOMEN

Nice figure, shapely, trim, well-proportioned.

FOR LARGER MEN

On the heavy side, large, brawny, burly, husky, stout.

FOR LARGER WOMEN

Queen-size, Rubenesque, voluptuous, slightly overweight, full-figured, plump, rounded, zaftig (comfortable and pleasingly plump).

EYES

FOR THOSE MEN WITH SPECIAL EYES

Blue-grey, steel blue, deep brown, green, devilish.

FOR THOSE WOMEN WITH SPECIAL EYES

Green, dark eyes, bedroom eyes, bewitching.

HAIR

FOR MEN WITH SPECIAL HAIR

Steel grey, silver, unruly, curly, sandy brown, black.

FOR WOMEN WITH SPECIAL HAIR

Red, auburn, blonde, strawberry blonde, black, brunette, long.

GENERAL APPEARANCE

FOR MEN

Handsome, Adonis, good-looking, easy on the eye, attractive, nice looking.

FOR WOMEN

Alluring, appealing, pretty, striking, stunning, gorgeous, cute, adorable, beautiful at times, nice looking, above average looks.

AGE

30 something, 30's, 39 Christmases, mid-40's, 40ish, fabulous fifty's, 60 +, and so on.

PERSONALITY CHARACTERIZATION

amusing	genuine	observant	urbane
audacious	genteel	passionate	visionary
brazen	honest	playful	warm
bright	humorous	quixotic	witty
caring	intelligent	romantic	X-rated
cheeky	jocular	sensuous	youthful
droll	keen	spiritual	zippy
energetic	loving	stable	
frisky	multi-faceted	tender	
fun-loving	nutty	toucher	

APPENDIX C

---

1. Imaginative Ads For Reviewing
2. Publications and Organizations

You are asked to complete the Ad Questionnaire (Appendix A, Form section) and on Line 8 you check the appropriate box, MARRIAGE, ROMANCE, FRIENDSHIP, COMPANIONSHIP, COME - OUT - AND - PLAY, and SOMETHING ELSE that best describes what you're looking for in a relationship. The ads below give you an idea of what others are writing. You will find this cross-section of ads and publications to be very interesting and instructive. The variety of the ads and the ingenuity of some of the writers show you the almost infinite number of ways you can accomplish the goal of finding the date/mate you want through the personals.

These ads were chosen because they are unique, creative, or unusual. Not all of them are well written, but they give you an idea of the immense diversity of personal ads across the country.

In the second section of this Appendix are listed a representative sampling of the publications and organizations involved in singles activities around the country. There are national, regional, local and some specialty publications. Most of these print personal ads and all of them can direct you to the singles organizations in their area.

You can advertise in publications with a national coverage (at a price), with a special subscriber base (such as art lovers, book lovers, airplane buffs, senior citizens.) or with regional or local coverage. Obviously, the great majority of advertisers want to meet their special person as close to home as possible. However, there are a few who select national or specialty coverage because they have special requirements, such as a desire to move, to travel, or to meet someone with a specific occupation.

IMAGINATIVE ADS FOR REVIEWING

MARRIAGE

Tall, Dark, and....

You be the judge. SWM, 29, 6'6", raised and educated back east. Pure ethics and morals. Athletically oriented. You name it, I probably like it. Searching for tall, trim woman to become my best friend and partner for life.

Loves Beautiful Blondes

DWM, intelligent, athletic, 43, looks younger. Has looks, money, seeks beautiful, slim happy lady, 26-34, kids OK, but no more.

Sensitive Communicator

SWM, 37, professional, healthy positive attitude, sensual, spiritual. I am looking for a special SWF, 23-35, under 5'5", attractive, feminine, metaphysical with high energy, self-esteem, common sense, a happy laugh and desire to start a family.

All Work and No Play

Isn't my idea of how I'd like to spend the rest of my life. Maybe you too are ready to meet someone who would like to experience fun times, romantic sunsets and real friendship that could last a lifetime.

Please Lord

Send me a LDS girl, with gospel values, not into makeup, jewelry, men's clothes. I'm 31, building my own company, into travel, camping, swimming and long walks together.

Family Man Wanted

Outgoing, assertive DWF, 39, mom, 5'4", skiing, dancing, camping. Seeks considerate, emotionally stable SWM, 37-45, sincere relationship.

Handsome, Tan, 175 lbs, 6', green eyes, sandy hair, athletic, ambitious. Seeks honest, petite SWF 19-20 for marriage.

ROMANCE

I Want To Fall In Love

SWF, 29, blonde/blue, slim, attractive and affectionate, NS, seeks successful, happy soulmate. Rollerblades, roller coasters, coffeehouses, books, travel and a sense of wonder and humor about the world preferred.

I'm A Kirstie Alley Type

5'5", 26, SWF/N, sexy, sophisticated, professional designer, looking for Mel Gibson's charisma, Kevin Costner's humility, Patrick Swayze's sensitivity, Tom Cruises's appeal, in an attractive, athletic, creative, witty, professional SWM/NS, 28-35, interested in real life, not acting the part.

Adventure, handsome, educated, honest, athletic, successful SWM 30 6'1", 185, NS/ND/drugs. Seeks attractive SF 23-35 for romance.

HANDSOME Black gent 30, 5'10", 180 seeks attractive, Black lady 21-31 for a close encounter relationship of the romantic kind.

FRIENDSHIP

Intriguing

Attractive SWF, 24, seeks tall, dark, stylish, artistic, creative SM, thinker for stimulating conversation. Friendship first, possible romance.

Searching For The Right

Chemistry! Loyalty, integrity and chivalry! If you are 45-50 call a petite brunette, DWF, who is witty, energetic, enjoys art, music, dancing and sincere friendship!

BIWF IN GOOD SHAPE

Attractive, clean, committed. Seeking same for open-minded fun and adventure, friendship.

COMPANIONSHIP

SWGM, 29, 5'9", 155 lbs

Average looking, non-smoker, sincere, quiet, and intelligent seeks similar male, 28-32, interesting in travel, movies, conversation and companionship. Not into bars or wildlife. A good attitude and sense of humor a must.

GWM, 36

150 lbs, smoker, enjoys beach, working out. Would like to meet men 40-50, straight appearing for mutual companionship. Straight appearing.

Active M, 68, leaving Mar 3 for Amsterdam-Brussels-Luxembourg-Paris. Cheaper to share a room with Female. No demands. Honorable.

LOVELY LAUGHING LADY!

Daughter seeks bright, stable, happy GENTLEMAN for fun, movies, dining, friendship with my attractive full-figured Mother. You're 50 plus, not marriage minded or short.

COME-OUT-AND-PLAY

BLUE EYES 6', fit male searching for girl 21 plus with right equipment: beach chair, bike, Buffet tapes, brains, passion, wine opener, open arms. I'm here!

STRICTLY FUN, recently separated, tall, dark, handsome, clean, WM, seeking beautiful, physical WF. No strings.

BEAUTIFUL Glider seeks strong tow plane, for soaring romance. ME: 30, 5'8", 135, pretty, loves flying, skiing, mtns. YOU: SDWM n-s, 28-42 in shape physically & emotionally.

SEEKING FUN

No commitment, attractive BM, 33, 6'2", 200 lbs businessman. Like spicy food, jazz, serious conversation, sports, works hard and needs to play. Seeking attractive women for fun.

'59 MENSANMOBILE

Chinese-Hungarian seeks lovable driver for interesting trip(s). Attractive blk/brn, with an interesting interior and a professionally written instruction book. Reasonable!

SOMETHING ELSE

RACQUETBALL

Beginner/intermediate level. SWM has court in WLA & S. Bay, need players, M/F, any age/race.

SWEET GAL, tall & slender, 29, seeks wanna-be cowboy partner for CW dance lessons. Intermediate or quick learner. Inquires welcome

HELP! My English is terrible. I'm 23 AF. If you are native speaker, 20-30, NS, let's converse. Dining, outings, movies.

F seeking F to form long relationship. Necessary: Age 25-35, feminist, anti-religion, pro-choice, anti-nuclear weapons, non-gay, must like men.

WHAT'S GOING ON HERE?

The following ads do not necessarily fit the Ad Questionnaire categories, but during my research I noticed a few of this type, so they are included.

Lovely, Lusty, Leggy, Oriental 20's, seeks generous financially secure, gentleman for mutually satisfying daytime erotic pleasures.

Blue - eyed feline blonde seeks long haired, sensual male. Passionate, healthy, creative.

Sexy, passionate, pretty, slender, blonde, seeks successful simple, Italian looking hard bodied guy 40 + to ignite ongoing romantic sparks.

Handsome, 6'3", 220 lbs, Black, athletic male, seeking generous mature WF or DWF for mutual fun and loving, etc. Only serious replies please. No men!

19 YEAR old SWM independent, seeks an older woman to show me the better things in life. Honest and very romantic, enjoys all outdoor activities.

PUBLICATIONS AND ORGANIZATIONS

ARIZONA

Single Scene
7432 E. Diamond St.
Scottsdale, AZ 85257-4031

Tucson Connection
P.O.Box 15114
Tucson, AZ 85708-0114

CALIFORNIA

Single Connections
P.O.Box 2527
Fullerton, CA 92633-0527

Trellis Singles Magazine
1260 Persian Dr., #6
Sunnyvale, CA 94089-2024

Orange County Register
P.O.Box 11626
Santa Ana, CA 92711

Los Angeles Times
Times Mirror Square
Los Angeles, CA 90053

Lifestyle
419 W. MacArthur Blvd.
Oakland, CA 94609-2808

Single in San Diego
P.O.Box 5709
San Diego, CA 92165-5709

Senior World of Orange County
7201 Garden Grove Blvd., Ste. K
Garden Grove, CA 92641

Get Personal
P.O.Box 256
Laguna Beach, CA 92651

Pacific Flyer
3355 Mission Ave., Ste. 213
Oceanside, CA 92054

COLORADO

Get-Two-Together
P.O.Box 1413
Ft. Collins, CO 80522-1413

Westword
P.O.Box 5970
Denver, CO 80217

Denver Post
1560 Broadway
Denver, CO 80202

Rocky Mountain News
400 W. Colfax Ave.
Denver, CO 80204

FLORIDA

1st Class Singles Lifestyle
219 E. Commercial Blvd.
Ft. Lauderdale, FL 33329-0297

Singles Serendipity
P.O.Box 5794
Jacksonville, FL 33308-4440

GEORGIA

Atlanta Singles Magazine
1780 Century Cir Ne #2
Atlanta, GA 30345-3020

ILLINOIS

Catholic Singles Magazine
901 S. Ashland Ave. #218
Chicago, IL 60607-4054

National Dating Scene
P.O.Box 1307
Skokie, IL 60607-4054

Chicago Life
P.O.Box 11311
Chicago, IL 60611-0311

MARYLAND

Cupid
P.O.Box 2531
Gaithersburg, MD 20879

Single Parent
8807 Colesville Rd
Silver Spring, MD 20910-4329

MASSACHUSETTS

Singles Almanac
138 Brighton Ave., #209
Boston, MA 02134-2830

Jewish Singles
P.O.Box 247
Newton, MA 02159-0002

MICHIGAN

Sincere Singles
P.O.Box 1719
Ann Arbor, MI 48106-1719

MISSOURI

Metro Singles
P.O.Box 28203
Kansas City, MO 64118-0203

NEVADA

True Match
P.O.Box 18000
Las Vegas, NV 89114

NEW JERSEY

Singles Journal
103 Cobblestone Ln
Cherry Hill, NJ 08003-2572

Homestead Hotline
720 Morrow Ave
Clayton, NJ 08312-2100

NEW MEXICO

On the Scene
3507 Wyoming Blvd., Ne
Albuquerque, NM 87111-4427

NEW YORK

Singles Almanac
80 E 11th St
New York, NY 10003-6000

Datebook
P.O.Box 473
Pleasantville, NY 10570-0473

Chocolate Singles
P.O.Box 333
Jamaica, NY 11413

Village Voice
842 Broadway
New York, NY 10003

The New York Review
250 West 57th St.
New York, NY 10107

OHIO

Singles Connection
P.O.Box 243
Cleveland, OH 44124-0388

PENNSYLVANIA

Lifestyles Pittsburgh
300 Mt. Lebanon Blvd.
Pittsburgh, PA 15234

TENNESSEE

Christian Single
127 9th Ave. N
Nashville, TN 37234-0001

TEXAS

U.S.Singles Today
P.O.Box 927
Bedford, TX 76095-0927

Touch of Class
12603 Prima Vista Dr.
San Antonio, TX 78233-6347

UTAH

Single Parent News
233 W. 200 10 N
Salt Lake City, UT 84103

WISCONSIN

Today's Single
1933 W. Wisconsin Ave.
Milwaukee, WI 53233-2001

NATIONAL

New York Magazine
P.O.Box 4600
New York, NY 10163

Art Lovers Network
P.O.Box 5106
Westport, CT 06881

Single Booklovers
Box 117
Gradyville, PA 19039

Health-Conscious Connections
P.O.Box 535
State College, PA 16804

National Singles Register
P.O.Box 567
Norwalk, CA 90650-0567

Index

ORDER FORM

POSTAL ORDERS: Baron Publications, P. O. Box 256,
Laguna Beach, CA 92651 USA.

Please send me "PERSONAL ADS - NEVER BE LONELY AGAIN" for the price of $12.95 per copy. I understand that I may return any of the copies for a full refund - for any reason - no questions asked.

When I purchase this book I understand that any checked items below will be forwarded to me at no further cost or obligation.

_____ Please send me a free sample of the GET PERSONAL newsletter.

_____ Please send me information on GET PERSONAL compatability testing.

_____ Please send me information on placing an ad in the GET PERSONAL newsletter.

Name:

Address:

City:

State: Zip Code:

SHIPPING: Book rate is $1.75 for the first book and $.75 for each additional book (Book rate shipping may take three to four weeks). Air Mail is $3.00 per book.

ORDER: No. of books_____ @ $12.95 $

      Shipping and handling

      Shipments to California add 7.75%

          Total - check enclosed with order $